1,000,000 Books

are available to read at

---◆---

www.ForgottenBooks.com

---◆---

Read online
Download PDF
Purchase in print

ISBN 978-0-282-35523-4
PIBN 10848728

This book is a reproduction of an important historical work. Forgotten Books uses
state-of-the-art technology to digitally reconstruct the work, preserving the original format
whilst repairing imperfections present in the aged copy. In rare cases, an imperfection in
the original, such as a blemish or missing page, may be replicated in our edition. We do,
however, repair the vast majority of imperfections successfully; any imperfections that
remain are intentionally left to preserve the state of such historical works.

Forgotten Books is a registered trademark of FB &c Ltd.
Copyright © 2018 FB &c Ltd.
FB &c Ltd, Dalton House, 60 Windsor Avenue, London, SW19 2RR.
Company number 08720141. Registered in England and Wales.

For support please visit www.forgottenbooks.com

1 MONTH OF
FREE
READING

at

www.ForgottenBooks.com

By purchasing this book you are eligible for one month membership to ForgottenBooks.com, giving you unlimited access to our entire collection of over 1,000,000 titles via our web site and mobile apps.

To claim your free month visit:
www.forgottenbooks.com/free848728

* Offer is valid for 45 days from date of purchase. Terms and conditions apply.

English
Français
Deutsche
Italiano
Español
Português

www.forgottenbooks.com

Mythology Photography **Fiction**
Fishing Christianity **Art** Cooking
Essays Buddhism Freemasonry
Medicine **Biology** Music **Ancient
Egypt** Evolution Carpentry Physics
Dance Geology **Mathematics** Fitness
Shakespeare **Folklore** Yoga Marketing
Confidence Immortality Biographies
Poetry **Psychology** Witchcraft
Electronics Chemistry History **Law**
Accounting **Philosophy** Anthropology
Alchemy Drama Quantum Mechanics
Atheism Sexual Health **Ancient History**
Entrepreneurship Languages Sport
Paleontology Needlework Islam
Metaphysics Investment Archaeology
Parenting Statistics Criminology
Motivational

Frontispiece   MEM SAHIB IN HER "PULL-MAN"

A CORNER IN INDIA

By

Mary Mead Clark

Philadelphia
American Baptist Publication Society
1907

Boston   Chicago   Atlanta
New York   St. Louis   Dallas

Frontispiece   MEM SAHIB IN HER "PULL-MAN"

A CORNER IN INDIA

By

Mary Mead Clark

Philadelphia
American Baptist Publication Society
1907
Boston   Chicago   Atlanta
New York   St. Louis   Dallas

BV3265
.C6

LIBRARY of CONGRESS
Two Copies Received
MAY 29 1907
Copyright Entry
Apr. 22, 1907
CLASS A XXc., No.
174647
COPY B.

Copyright 1907 by the
AMERICAN BAPTIST PUBLICATION SOCIETY

Published May, 1907

TO
My Husband
AND FRIENDS IN THIS AND OTHER LANDS
WHOSE PRAYERS AND LOVE AND INTEREST
HAVE BEEN OUR CONSTANT INSPIRATION
THESE MANY YEARS; AND TO THE YOUNG
MEN AND WOMEN WHO ARE NEEDED TO
FURTHER PLANT THE BANNER OF THE
CROSS AMONG SAVAGE TRIBES

" Mine album is the savage breast,
Where darkness broods and tempests rest
Without one ray of light;
To write the name of Jesus there,
And point to worlds all bright and fair,
And see the savage bow in prayer,
Is my supreme delight."

PREFACE

IN the preparation of this little volume we have been encouraged and inspired by many helpful suggestions from our former colaborers in the distant wilds, Rev. F. P. Haggard, Corresponding Secretary of the American Baptist Missionary Union, and Dr. W. E. Witter, District Secretary for New England.

It is sent forth with the earnest prayer that the young men and women who may chance to read it will not only be entertained, but moved to action in behalf of the savage tribes whose habits, customs, and possibilities are here depicted from personal observation through many years.

MARY MEAD CLARK.

AMENIA, N. Y., 1907.

INTRODUCTION

WHILE Doctor Clark continues his personal ministry to the wild tribes of Assam, among which he has spent so many years of self-sacrificing service, it will be a pleasure to many in America and across the seas to read the racy glimpses of life among the warlike Nagas by Mrs. Clark who, after sharing so long the perils of these frontier experiences, is now detained in America.

We especially commend this interesting narrative to the hosts of young people, many of whom are almost persuaded that the heroic in missions is forever passed. Let them follow some of those distant mountain paths, cross the steep ravines and swollen rivers, face the wild tribes still waiting for the gospel, and marvel at what God has wrought among those who have received the message. They will then thank the author for her thrilling story, and some will not be slow to say, "Lord, here am I; send me"; while every reader will be sure to pray, "To such a harvest, Lord, thrust forth the laborers."

This is a fine book for vacation reading. It smells of the forests, kindles the imagination, warms the heart, is better than a novel, for it is not only full of romance, but is true.

WILLIAM ELLSWORTH WITTER.

FORD MEMORIAL BUILDING
BOSTON, MASS., June, 1906

CONTENTS

LIST OF ILLUSTRATIONS

A Corner in India

HILL TRIBES OF ASSAM

"I DON'T want the goat! I don't want it! I will not have it! Take it away, take it away," was reiterated again and again; yet these strange, uncivilized men, down from their mountain fastnesses, still persisted in dragging up the steps of the veranda of our bungalow a large, long-horned hill goat, hoping to receive from us double or quadruple its value, and nothing short of landing it inside the house would satisfy them. Thus was I introduced to these stalwart, robust warriors, dressed mostly in war medals, each man grasping his spear shaft decorated with goat's hair, dyed red and yellow, and also fringed with the long black hair of a woman, telling the story of bloody deeds.

As I looked for the first time into the hard faces of these hill people, dubbed by the Assamese "head cutters," how little I thought that soon our commodious, pleasant bungalow, with its garden and its flowers, situated on the bank of the artificial lake at Sibsagor

(Sib's or Siva's Ocean), would be left for a home in a small bamboo mat house in the mountain wilds.

But first, ere we enter this hill country, a few words about Assam. Originally it was the valley of the Brahmaputra River, and for the last three-quarters of a century has been a part of the great empire of India. An alluvial plain of great fertility, about fifteen hundred miles in length, with an average breadth of fifty miles, it extends to the extreme northeast of India, touching Tibet and Burma and reaching far toward China. It is peopled by various races of Aryan and Mongolian stock, which differ widely in customs, language, and religion.

Although Assam lies wholly within the temperate zone, its climate partakes of that of the tropics, ranging from forty degrees to one hundred degrees Fahrenheit, with an average of seventy-five degrees. The atmosphere is very humid, and the annual rainfall about one hundred inches. This heavy precipitation upon an extremely fertile soil causes excessive vegetable growth and decay, and induces, as would be expected, much malaria and fever. Cherra Punji, an exposed point in the hills, has some four hundred and eighty-nine inches of rain yearly, the largest known rainfall in the world.

Far away in the distant blues are the fountain-heads of the numerous streams which lave and enrich this valley. The mighty Brahmaputra—the great highway for trade and travel—plowing down through the entire length of this rich, fertile plain of Assam, cuts it in twain. As the mountains are round about Jerusalem, so, hemming in this beautiful valley, are the lower ranges of the Himalayas, populated by numerous sturdy and savage tribes.

The majority of the valley people are Hindus and Mohammedans. Here and there statues of Buddha are found carved on rocks and temples. The religion of the hill tribes is animism, or demon worship, tinctured in very rare instances with Buddhism.

The tea industry of Assam has created an enormous demand for labor, supplied mostly by thousands of Kolarian immigrants from Central India, who are derisively known as Kols (pigs). In this rude population —largely demon-worshipers—is found a virgin soil, the richest in all this valley for gospel seed-sowing.

Beginning at the western extremity, along the north side of the valley on the sub-hills of the eternal snow-capped Himalayas, are the homes of the Bhutanese, the Akhas, the Daphlas, Miris, Abors, and Mishmis. The last hold, it is believed, a comparatively easy pass into Tibet. Their trade route reaches Sadiya, the first mission station in Assam. At the head of this valley China-ward is the large tribe of Khamtis (Shans), to labor for whom there came from Burma in 1835 Rev. Nathan Brown, D. D., as preacher and translator, and Mr. O. T. Cutter, with a printing press, as publisher and general helper. Passing the Khamtis, we come to the large Dehing River, through whose valleys and gorges, in the cool season, people from Northern Burma and the borders of China come into Assam for trade. By this route, early in the thirteenth century, came the Ahoms, who dominated Assam for five hundred years, and from whom the province is supposed to derive its name (Ahom-Assam?). By this route also came the Burmese when they invaded and despoiled Assam, a little previous to the English occupation of this territory, in 1826.

Through this Assam valley to upper Burma and China surveys have recently been made to connect the railways of Bengal with those of Burma. This region is now occupied by the Singphos, who on the Burma side are called Kachins. To the southwest next below the Singphos are found the various tribes of Nagas, who, with other people of like character, reach from fifty to one hundred and fifty miles across the watershed into Burma, the Nagas stretching along the southern boundary of upper Assam two hundred and fifty miles or more. On a spur from these hills are located the Mikirs, for whom the American Baptist Missionary Union is working; and farther on are the Jaintas and Khasias, where is the very successful work of the Welsh Presbyterians. Adjoining these, and bordering on Bengal, are the Garos, where long has been the banner mission of American Baptists in Assam. Still other hill tracts are peopled by large tribes of the same aboriginal stock, who have yet to hear the first notes of the gospel of peace.

SIBSAGOR TREASURY, COURTHOUSE, AND TEMPLES

Page 5

BEGINNINGS AMONG THE NAGAS

IN 1838-1841 Rev. Miles Bronson began work among the Singphos and Nagas. He prepared a spelling book for each of these people, also a catechism in the Naga language. He went into the hills with his family, but was obliged, after a few months, to leave on account of illness, lack of suitable food, and accommodations. An old chief came, bringing his sons, and said: " Go, get well, come again, but before your return I shall be gone. My hair is ripe, yet here are my sons, who will stand pledged to be your friends." By the early removal of the mission from Jaipur to Sibsagor and Nowgong work among that tribe of Nagas was suspended, and the descendants of the old chief have not to this day had the privilege of redeeming the pledge to stand by the missionary.

A man from Merangkong, a village in the Ao Naga tribe, while living in Sibsagor was baptized in 1851 by Rev. S. M. Whiting. This man while on a visit to his native village was killed in a hostile attack. This is all that was done toward giving the gospel to the Nagas previous to the undertaking of Mr. Clark.

In October, 1868, with Mrs. Simons, a missionary returning to her husband in Burma, we left Boston in the bark " Pearl," a trading vessel of three hundred tons burden, bound for Calcutta via the Cape of Good Hope. During our voyage of one hundred and sixty days we put into no ports, sighted no land, were indeed prisoners on the deep, subject to the storms and hardships incident to a winter on board a small trading vessel. For hardtack and bacon, plum duff and salt junk, " lights and sounds," we lost our relish. The water, shipped from Boston for the voyage, grew thick, then grew thin, and oh, the odor! " Too scrupulous," the sailors said when we refused to drink it, but joyfully reveled with us in occasional fresh draughts from the clouds.

When our little cockle-shell habitation was tossed like a football by angry waves, dashing and breaking and flooding the decks, while mingled with their roar and dash we heard the dragging of ropes and Captain Harding's command, " Close reef sail, stand by the main halyards," we were in no mood to write of the awful grandeur of a storm at sea. We could do that better later with a steadier hand.

Occasionally the spouting of a whale in the distance or a full view of this floating monster, or the pulling in of a dolphin or a shark, broke the monotony of our daily life. At times we almost prayed for wings when flocks of albatross, rising from the waters and soaring majestically heavenward, seemed to mock us on our sea-bound craft. Great navigators we became, locating our position from day to day in the ship's chart, and mighty astronomers too—why not, with the unbroken starry expanse and no lack but instruments! But how tame was everything else compared with sighting and speaking other vessels, inquiring by signals whence and whither bound, and what their last word from the land world; and if, perchance, we saw "old glory" hoisted, how our ocean home resounded with the genuine three cheers!

In due time we reached " far India's shores," and after a few days' sight-seeing and shopping in Calcutta and a few hours of railway we boarded a snail-like traffic steamer for the long, tedious journey up the turbid waters of the crooked, winding Brahmaputra. We " tied up " to the river bank each night and pulled out mornings at " the lifting of the fog." From fifteen to twenty days, and not unusually twenty-five, were consumed on the upward trip. In consequence of cholera on board we made our trip in fourteen days.

Her Majesty's mail, too progressive for these slow boats, was " backed " the entire distance from Calcutta through Assam by relays of running coolies. Now comfortable little mail steamers ply these waters.

In the travelers' bungalow at Dikho Mukh (mouth of the Dikho River) we passed a comfortless night with rats and cockroaches, and in wakeful fear of snakes and centipedes. We closed the glassless windows by drawing the hanging mats across the openings, and piled our trunks and boxes against the doors.

The next morning several miles by elephant through

the jungle brought us to a point on the Dikho River
where we found a native boat sent down by Doctor
Ward, of Sibsagor. The trunks of two large trees dug
out, supporting a bamboo platform, furnished a deck
on which a miniature house for cabin was built of
bamboos and canvas. Our motive power was natives,
who, thrusting long bamboo poles into the bank, ran
one after another the length of our deck. How wild,
and strange, and fascinating withal that journey!

At a native village, where we tied up, a heathen festival and worship was in progress, and all night long
the din of drums, the blowing of horns, weird shout-
ings to wake up the gods, together with the responses
of yelling jackals, hooting owls, and screaming monkeys, made confusion worse confounded. When within
eight miles of Sibsagor we mounted ponies sent to
meet us, and gladly galloped in, thus ending our long
journey. Mr. Clark was sent out as superintendent of
the Mission Press, and also to relieve temporarily in
general mission work Rev. W. Ward, D. D., then about
to take a much-needed furlough in America.

Our first home faced a beautiful little sheet of water
encircled by a delightful drive of just two miles. On a
raised embankment of this Sibsagor "tank" are the
English court house, the treasury building, the resi-
dences of the English officials and the mission bungalow; but most picturesque of all are three very fine
symmetrically built heathen temples. However, that
we might be nearer the printing press and our work

generally, we soon located in an old bungalow on the bank of the Dikho River, about a half-mile away.

As each cold season came around hill men came in for trade and sight-seeing. Our press building, with its typesetting, printing, and binding of books was for them the wonder of wonders. Some of the great men, dressed in their military costumes, came one day to our schoolhouse door and, manifesting much interest in what we were doing, were asked, " Wouldn't you like us to come up to your village and teach your children as you see these being taught?" A chief replied, " Yes, and we will send our children to learn." " But we hear that you take heads up there." " Oh, yes, we do," he replied, and seizing a boy by the head gave us in a quite harmless way an object-lesson of how they did it.

From the broad veranda of the mission bungalow we looked out day after day, on and on beyond the villages, across the rice fields, over the jungles of the plains, upon the mountains towering in silent grandeur against the southern sky, as if watching for the feet of him who bringeth good tidings that publisheth peace; and with our own Doctor Brown we could say:

> My soul is not at rest; there comes a strange
> And secret whisper to my spirit . . .

and we told our Assamese Christians how we longed to bear the message to those distant wilds. They shook their heads doubtfully. " They are savages,

sahib, village warring with village, constantly cutting
off heads to get skulls." But my husband replied:

> "The voice of my departed Lord,
> 'Go teach all nations' . . .
>   Comes on the night air and awakes my ear,
>   And I *will* go."

Our ardent Godhula, Assamese evangelist and school
teacher, full of tact and courage, caught the spirit of
advance and volunteered to make the first venture.
Earnest, wrestling prayer was answered. A Naga man
living near Sibsagor was persuaded to come evenings
to Godhula's house, and while he talked about his people Godhula listened with open ears and soon could
speak a little of the language.

When the cold season of 1871 came around Godhula,
with his Naga companion, started out for the tea gardens lying along the base of the hills, with orders from
Mr. Clark to go no further if to do so would be at too
great risk.

At Amguri Tea Gardens, Godhula met many men
from Dekha Haimong village and shared with them his
own finer rice, smoked and talked with them, and gradually gained their confidence. But when he proposed
to accompany them to their village home, ah! that was
a different matter. None of the "tartars" (village officials) were with them, and what right had they to
bring a "subject man," "a Company man" (one living
under English rule) into their territory? But God-

hula was not easily shaken off. "Well, come along then; we'll guard you on the way, but when we get there all must be as the tartars say." One night's lodging in the forest, and the second day brought the party to Dekha Haimong village.

Godhula proclaimed himself as teacher of a new religion, and declared this to be his sole errand. But his motives were impugned. "What do we want of this man's new religion?" exclaimed one of the chief men, among the first to espouse the cause later on. "Send him off," "Get him out of the way," "A spy, doubtless, of the 'Company,'" exclaimed others.

A small rude hut was assigned to Godhula and a guard appointed to watch him closely. For two or three days not a man, woman, or child would go near his house. But when with his deep-toned, melodious voice he poured out his soul in the sweet gospel hymns in Assamese the people flocked around him and listened as he told them, in his own eloquent way, the sweet old, old story. Jesus and heaven were names now heard for the first time. The people coming up from their day's work at evening were conscious of a new, a different atmosphere. The influence of peace and love began to soften their hard hearts, and they called this rude grass hut "the sweet home," the peaceful place. Soon the bands which made Godhula a prisoner were loosed and the freedom of the village was his. Famine, pestilence, and war, involving many and costly sacrifices to secure the favor of the deities, had

so impoverished the people that many were having
scarcely one good meal a day. In the failure of their
own gods to give them help they were all the more
ready to listen concerning Him, who, Godhula told
them, was the Bread of Life. The great straits to
which this village was reduced was thus under God
the occasion by which a man was found in the plains
as guide and a door opened to the hearts of the people.

When Godhula proposed to return to Sibsagor
women and children wept, and to do him proper honor
an escort of forty men was sent by the authorities of
the village to accompany him to the door of the mission
bungalow in Sibsagor. These men seated on our
veranda were a picturesque and interesting sight, and
far-reaching and full of meaning was our conference
with them concerning future visits.

In April, 1872, Godhula and his wife, Lucy, a former
pupil in Mrs. Whiting's school, started for the hills to
remain through the rains. This was a bold venture.
No one from civilization had before attempted it. On
account of the difficulty of communication with the
plains in the wet season, we seldom heard from them,
but they were held before the throne in many prayers
by the missionaries and the Christians at Sibsagor.

The Nagas built a small bamboo chapel for religious
services, and much instruction was given in the new
religion. The reward was almost immediate. In November Godhula came down from his mountain aerie,
bringing with him the first-fruits of faithful labor.

Even cholera in the plains, which the Nagas greatly dread, did not deter these new disciples.

It was a touching, solemn scene in our mission chapel at Sibsagor when these wild men, battle-axe and spear in hand, with stammering tongues tried to tell in broken Assamese, with help in as imperfect Naga from their teacher, of this newly found Saviour, and of their desire to follow in his ordinances. Not infrequently as one hesitated in relating his experience the one next to him, having perhaps a little larger Assamese vocabulary, would come to his aid. Nine were received, and on the following Sabbath, on profession of their faith in Christ, were buried in baptism in the Dikho River in front of the mission bungalow. " It is all light! " " It is all light! " was their joyful exclamation when later we gathered around the table of our Lord.

These Naga Christians, now very desirous of taking Mr. Clark up to their mountain home, and having no calendar save the wet and dry season, seed time and harvest, and the moon's changes, fixed upon a certain phase of the next moon as the date when they would come and take him up to their savage wilds. At the appointed time sixty warriors appeared to escort him.

The first night Mr. Clark spent with the hospitable English tea planter, Colonel Buckingham, at Amguri Tea Garden. The second night overtook the travelers in the dense, shelterless forest, but with plenty of tree branches and leaves at hand snug lodgings rose like magic. All night the Nagas lay toasting their feet around the campfire. This seemed to compensate for proper covering. Sentinels kept watch by turns, as here was an all too inviting prey for wild beasts and human enemies as well. For additional security the space around was made to bristle with pongees (small bamboo spikes) stuck in the ground. En route everything was done for the safety of my husband, and during his stay in the village no service was withheld which would in anywise contribute to his welfare.

During this venture beyond the British flag and postal service no intelligence could be received from Mr. Clark; and not infrequently I was asked by the chief magistrate of Sibsagor Station, " When have you last heard from Mr. Clark? " " Do you ever expect to see your husband back with his head on his shoulders? " I need not say I was solicitous, yet from the heart there ever came the answer: " Yes, Colonel Campbell, I expect him back with his head on; I trust to a higher power than the English government to keep my husband's head on his shoulders."

III

A PLUNGE INTO BARBARISM

"I BELIEVE I have found my life-work," exclaimed Mr. Clark as he entered the old press bungalow on his return from his twelve days' absence in the wilds of barbarism.

During the three subsequent years Godhula and his wife lived a part of each year at Dekha Haimong village, to which Mr. Clark made occasional visits. But to the missionary, three days from his now chosen field, with no facilities for acquiring the language, the prosecution of the work was difficult and unsatisfactory.

Doctor Ward, returning from America about this time, eager for the work of Bible translation for which he was so richly endowed, soon closed the Book below to receive the Author's " Well done " above; and his grave beside the native Christians to this day remains a sacred memorial of his love for them and his silent call " to follow in his train." Rev. A. K. Gurney was sent to carry on the work laid down by Doctor Ward, and soon after his arrival Mr. Clark, so long burdened for the Nagas, reported himself at Dekha Haimong in the Hills, March, 1876.

To live beyond the English flag at that time required a permit from the Viceroy of India, residing in Cal-

cutta. On making application Mr. Clark received the
reply that should he enter the Naga wilds he must do
it at his own risk, with no expectation whatever of
protection from British arms. The English government was still smarting from the recent rout of a
large survey party sent to reconnoiter this territory
and the brutal murder of Captain Butler with one of his
native soldiers. But the call, " Go teach all nations,"
and the promise, " Lo, I am with you alway," nerved
my husband to brave all perils that he might there
plant the banner of the cross. Taking with him only
the most necessary articles, he was soon settled in part
of a Naga house, the luxuriance of which demanded a
rental of about thirty cents a month. His cook and
general housekeeper was an orphan Bengali lad, who
had been our ward for some time at Sibsagor. No in-
ducement could have persuaded an Assamese servant to
accompany him. There in a crowded village, fortified
by a heavy stockade, was begun the mining of this
unwritten language and the necessary deeper delving
to unearth the real character of these new parishioners. At first it was a presumptuous venture to go far
outside the village stockade, not only on account of
lurking enemies, but because of numerous hidden pongees, to step upon which would occasion severe, if not
fatal, wounds. Far removed from everything approaching music, the sound of the huge drum—the
Naga tocsin—calling the people from cultivation or
jungle, was not an unwelcome sound.

NAGA MEN IN ORDINARY COSTUME

The little band of disciples, with a few others favorably inclined toward the new religion, mostly men, met together from Sabbath to Sabbath to discuss with Mr. Clark " the power-filled doctrine," and one and another convert witnessed his symbolic resurrection to newness of life in those mountain streams. But Satan was not idle. The village was divided regarding this new order of things and far from one mind in permitting the continued residence of this white-faced foreigner. Neighboring villages were saying, " You will find sooner or later that this great rajah preacher is a disguised agent of ' The Company.' " " Has he not the same white face? " Glorying in their independence, these savage hill men were utterly opposed to any movement that foreshadowed in the least any alliance whatever with this great and ever-encroaching power. Adherents of the old, cruel faith were quick to see that the gospel of peace and love would rapidly empty their skull houses and put to rout most of the old customs handed down from forefathers, for whom they held the greatest reverence. The missionary's presence and his teachings had spread like wildfire from mountain peak to mountain peak and everywhere was fostered the suspicious spirit.

Two of Dekha Haimong's young men of promise, just entering official ranks, had come out for Christ and were already veritable Aarons and Hurs to the missionary. Hostility to the new religion waxed stronger and stronger. There was a division in the village

B

councils; repeated efforts were made by the opponents
of Christianity to inveigle their village into war with
other villages, and thus to overwhelm by a strong war
spirit the influence of the few Christians, whose teachings were so antagonistic to their military ambition,
without the realization of which there could be for
them no social or political standing in the community,
and for which they would willingly imperil life.   To
intimidate the missionary, a war party of young men
ambushed one whole week for human heads, which
they intended to throw down before him as symbolical
of what he might expect himself in case he did not
retreat to the plains.   They returned, however, without
booty, but racked with fever, thus affording the missionary an opportunity of exercising some medical skill
and taming their savagery.

IV

THE tillable lands about Dekha Haimong were limited and had been much exhausted by frequent croppings. The prospect was poverty rather than a promise of comfortable maintenance by agriculture. Some three hours' march away was a good village site, occupied years ago by a people which had been destroyed and scattered through repeated wars. Dekha Haimong had for years considered a removal to this Molung crest, so rich in promise of abundant harvests, and now the adherents of the new faith, persecuted at home, determined to put into execution this long-mooted project.

According to Naga usage, the foster-parent village of Dekha Haimong, named Sungdia, must be consulted. It, of course, disapproved, and, so far as lay in its power, tried in every way to prevent the separation. This delay only brought additional vexation and harassment to the little band of colonists which desired peace and the opportunity of worshiping according to the dictates of their own enlightened consciences. One hundred men from Merangkong, a friendly village a day's march distant, proposing to join this new enterprise, it was decided to make the move at once, as it was fully expected if

a start were only made Dekha Haimong, seeing the
advantages of the new location, would soon follow
en masse, and the Christians, having been leaders in
the enterprise, would be in the ascendancy in the new
colony. So on the day appointed the missionary, with
fifteen families, bearing on their backs all of their own
and the missionary's household goods, marched down
through the gateway of Dekha Haimong stockade
amid the jeers, taunts, scoffs, and threats of the villagers, who shouted, " Go now, but you'll soon come
back," and one man posing astride the gateway of the
stockade indicated to them the humility and greater
subjection under which they would return.

Molung peak was then a dense wilderness, the haunt
of elephants, tigers, leopards, and lesser foes. The
new-comers arrived on the ground late in the afternoon
of October 24, 1876, and for two nights the beautiful
starry canopy was their only shelter. Watch fires were
kept burning day and night, and yet they could not be
allowed to blaze too brightly lest this attempt at a new
settlement be discovered by the many villages crowning other peaks, which, always desirous of contrib-
uting to their skull-houses, would at once make a raid
on this helpless little community. To avoid such exposure their first huts of grass were built with roofs
slanting to the ground in the rear and open only toward
the plain of Assam in order to avoid any show of fire
Naga-hillward, and Mr. Clark's cook was repeatedly
warned not to give much blaze to his fire.

Then followed the work of clearing the forest for building sites. Right here on the ground were posts, reeds, bamboo for walls and flooring, thatch for roofing, and houses began to go up rapidly. One afternoon men set to work on a house for Mr. Clark, and it was ready for occupancy the same evening. It was very small and Naga-like in architecture, intended only as a temporary provision until the families should be housed, when larger accommodations were promised; but, owing to difficulties which soon followed, this hut was his only home for upwards of four months.

The new settlers were disappointed in the non-arrival of the expected quota from Merangkong. That village, having many wars on hand, feared so large a reduction of its forces, and "shut the door" against the removal of the one hundred, and only a few families were permitted to leave. Dekha Haimong village, instead of joining the emigrants, as was anticipated, renewed its hostility, thinking thereby to force back to the old home those who had sought to escape its tyranny. They carried their bitterness so far as to go long distances in different directions endeavoring to instigate other villages to assail the little Christian band alone in the wilderness.

The opening up of the crest of the hill by clearing land round about for the rice cultivation and burning the felled trees and jungle telegraphed to other mountain peaks around the existence of this new settlement. All sorts of rumors were now rife of the proposed attack of this or that strong village, against which they knew there could be no chance for defense. Even Sungdia village, the friend and protector of the mother village, Dekha Haimong, sent a messenger direct to this child of its ward to say that it was not worth while to expend much labor on houses or in preparing land for crops, as the former would soon be in ashes and the latter grown up to jungle, and that the white man's blood would flow quite as easily as that of the sturdy mountaineer. Then came the test; was their protector for many years now to be their enemy? Sungdia had too brilliant a war record for such a message to be disregarded; the situation grew more alarming; it would be hazardous in the extreme for such a handful of unprotected ones to try to maintain themselves in a country such as this, where badges of honor are bestowed as a premium for human heads. What was to be done? Many consultations between the missionary and the people were held. Mr. Clark, in view of the circumstances, advised a return to the home village, there to stand up for Christ and their rights, spiritual and temporal. "No," came the reply, "we will never go back to so bad a rule and such vexatious persecution; we will go with you, 'father,' to the plains of Assam, anywhere you will, but never back to Dekha Haimong."

At last, after much thought, conference, and prayer, messengers were despatched to this threatening village with, in substance, the following: "We remember,

Sungdia, with much gratitude your kindness to the Dekha Haimong people, of whom we are a part. Time and again have you fought for us when in peril; we have only thankful hearts to you-ward. We desire most earnestly to perpetuate the pleasant relations of the past, and to remain under your parental watch-care. A little handful of us have come off from Dekha Haimong to form a new community, where we may worship in peace and quiet the one true God, of whom we have so recently heard. He is the great God who made heaven and earth and all things. Heretofore success has ever crowned your arms, but you cannot fight against the great Jehovah. Beware, we as your loving children entreat you. The white man's object here is to give you the very richest of blessings; for this only has he come; believe this."

On the reception of this verbal communication, this big war village, that had never known defeat, made reply after three days' conference that there had been many false rumors, misrepresentations, and much misunderstanding, and now Sungdia not only avowed its friendship in strong terms, but pledged its protection and support to this new venture. This gave much relief.

In the apparent hedging up of Christianity in Dekha Haimong village there was much earnest prayer that some way might be opened for the extension of Christ's kingdom among these hill tribes. Was the planting of this new colony the beginning of a people for the Lord in these mountain wilds? The missionary resolved to stand by this people, to throw in his lot with them, trusting in the Lord alone for protection. More permanent houses went up rapidly, work on the rice lands went forward. Dekha Haimong was now convinced of the settled determination of this offshoot, and one family after another gradually joined the enterprise, but there was no coming over en masse.

The new village was formed without the accustomed heathen ceremonies to propitiate demons by great and expensive sacrificial offerings. It was determined to abandon aggressive warfare and to be known as a peaceable, Christian village, the first to have this appellation in all this wild mountain region stretching from the valley of the Brahmaputra far away across the hills to the plains of Burma. There was, however, to be no law preventing others who might join this new community from worshiping as they chose, "no law to make Christians"; but the standard of the cross was erected, the gospel of salvation from sin through Jesus Christ alone was proclaimed, and his followers were to be allowed to worship unmolested the one true God.

Prospects had now assumed a decidedly more hopeful aspect, and on my return from America, much recruited in health, I was permitted by the English government to join my husband in this independent hill territory. In anticipation of this coming the village authorities set the whole working force of the village repairing and enlarging the mission house, volunteering one week's work gratis, meanwhile questioning, "Why, father, there are to be only two of you; how can two people live in so many rooms?" (Three rooms and a storeroom!)

V

" AS Mr. Clark has been able to keep his head on,
now we will try yours," Colonel Campbell, chief
magistrate of Sibsagor district, facetiously remarked
to me on my return to Sibsagor from America, en
route for Molung, Naga Hills.

Our former mission home at Sibsagor, then occupied
by our successors, Rev. and Mrs. Gurney, was still to
be a refuge in case of emergency, as there was not yet
sufficient confidence in the security of our new abode
to move all of our belongings thither. Fire or foe
might make short work of our possessions. A village
going up in flame and smoke was no uncommon sight.

An elephant, and bullock carts had been previously
engaged for the transportation of ourselves and luggage the twenty-two miles to Amguri, at the foot of
the hills. One mile from Sibsagor station we crossed
the Dikho River and entered royal grounds formerly
occupied by the kings of Assam. This broad tract of
level land, once covered by hundreds of native houses,
is now largely grown up to jungle. That portion
devoted exclusively to the royal family, embracing an
area of many acres, was enclosed by two parallel brick
walls, within which were the king's palace, treasury,

26

and guard house. Their arched roofs, outer and inner walls, and floors are of heavy brick masonry, noble relics of ancient days. In these solid walls and floors excavations, large and deep, have been made in search for the kings' jewels and treasures supposed to have been buried there. A little outside the walled enclosure, located on the embankment of an excavated lake, is a fine temple of chaste, symmetrical proportions, named for the wife of one of the old kings, Joyhagor, *hagor* meaning ocean, really Joy's ocean. A short distance in another direction, still in very good repair, is the Rong-ghor (king's playhouse). Surrounding this was a high wall, within which there were enacted plays, games, and contests with wild beasts for the entertainment of the royal family.

Leaving these interesting reminders of the olden days, we exchanged the comfortable, civilized conveyance of pony and cart loaned us by Colonel Campbell for the barbarous swing-swang gait of the elephant. Eight miles by our pachyderm under the piercing rays of a midday tropical sun, and we were glad to find a pony and dog cart from Colonel Buckingham, Amguri, awaiting us at another heathen temple.

We soon reached the grand highway, Ladiaghur, a splendid road of eight or ten feet elevation, thrown up by one of the old Assam kings. All the great trunk roads of Assam were built by these ancient rulers, and are now kept in repair by the government. Branching off from this great highway we entered Amguri Tea

Estate, and through a long avenue of nahor trees, beautiful in their varied hues and shades, we arrived at the fine, spacious bungalow of this flourishing tea garden, comprising thousands of acres and giving employment to thirty thousand people. We wandered through the paths of this beautiful estate, visited the tea houses, and were shown the varied processes by which the leaf is prepared for the cup that cheers.

As the native Assamese is quite satisfied with the support which his patch of rice or little bazaar affords, the tea planters, at considerable expense, bring annually from Chota-Nagpur and other provinces of India thousands of laborers to serve on their gardens. These coolies come with their all tied up in little bundles suspended from bamboo poles and borne across their shoulders. They usually make a five years' agreement under government supervision, and very frequently reenlist for a second or third term; their children in the meantime become helpers in leaf-plucking and receive free schooling. In time many take up lands of their own and become rice cultivators.

One evening we went to a little settlement of houses on the outskirts of a garden, where we found a crowd gathered around one of our own missionaries, who was explaining the pictures from home Sunday-school lesson rolls. It was beautiful to watch the look of rest stealing over those bronzed faces as they caught the message, " Come unto me all ye that labor."

To continue our journey hillward, early the second

COLONEL BUCKINGHAM'S BUNGALOW

day the Naga Hills "goods train" arrived, men and women in large numbers, each bringing a native basket to be filled or the bark band to attach to a piece of luggage, all of which had to be arranged in parcels not exceeding about sixty pounds. The contents of heavy trunks were turned into the baskets, the trunks taken empty or nearly so. Five of the strongest men were detailed as my "Pullman" (pullmen), one at a time for my bamboo chair. The chief men, village officials, were also on hand, not to carry loads, oh, no! this would be much beneath their dignity; they were here to give honor to the occasion. Surely never was a queen more revered by her subjects than was now the wife of the Naga Hills' missionary by his parishioners.

When all was ready, each man "backed" his chosen piece of luggage held by the bark band passing across his forehead. My chair was carried in the same manner; the whole presenting a long and decidedly picturesque procession. A half-hour brought us to the Jhanzi, crossing which we bade good-by to civilization. I kept to my chair as my ferry, while my husband's passage over was by a Naga's back without a chair. The Naga burden-bearing song with response, "Oh-hee! Hee hoh! Ha-hee, Ho-hum! Halee-he, Ho-hum!" with repetition and variation, now sounding on my ears for the first time, was indeed very musical.

Our route was simply a Naga trail, first across the lowlands where grow in such profusion the tall, feathery, waving bamboos, intertwined and interlaced, forming pretty, fantastic arbors across our path, and not infrequently necessitating the cutting of our way. On and on we went, up and down the lower hills, crossing mountain streams, through forests of stately trees with delicate creepers entwining their giant trunks, their branches gracefully festooned with vines, and orchids swaying in the breeze. For all ages past, unobserved and unappreciated, this wilderness of beauty has budded and put forth, only to delight the eyes of Him who makes even the desert to blossom as the rose.

Frequent and numerous traces of wild elephants, tigers, and bears, and the chatter of monkeys forcibly reminded us that we were penetrating the regions beyond—were truly pioneers of a new enterprise. We were fast adding new and interesting experiences. I occasionally alighted from my chair for a little walk, a relief to my bearers as well as myself, but it was very certain that the long skirts from New York dressmakers were never intended for jungle paths and the crossing of deep ravines on a single tree trunk.

My attention was directed to a precipitous descent on the left of our path, where, not long before, a party ambushing just above swooped down upon some travelers, leaving twenty-five bodies headless.

With sharpened appetites we reached the Taero, a clear, rapid stream, and a favorite Naga lunching place. Seated on a clean rock, how romantic, how wild, how picnicky it seemed! European, Assamese, and Naga each partook of his own particular food, we from our lunch basket, the Nagas from a bright, glossy leaf tied with a rattan. Such a pretty glimpse of the valley of Assam down through the forest! While we were resting, some of our traveling companions were smoking, some scouring their brass and shell ornaments in the sand, others taking a bath in the stream below, and still others doing a little laundering.

But hark! We were aroused by the " Hi-ho, Hai-hum! " and the rattling of battle-axes in the distance. Some of our party went forward to learn whether friends or foes were approaching. The response came back, " All is well," and soon two hundred men, traders, each with spear and battle-axe, passed by en route to the plain. Our train moved on again, the path rapidly grew steeper, the burden-bearing song louder and deeper accordingly.

On a little open plateau, our procession came to a halt, and some one started a fire. We exclaimed, " Why, we are not going to eat again! " " No, only make a smoke to notify the village that we are coming." Naga telegraphy! and that too, wireless, has been practised here for ages! In due time the message was answered by young men and maidens coming hurry-scurry down the mountain steeps with bark bands and baskets to divide the loads and relieve their friends. Steeper and steeper, rockier and more rocky grew our path, men actually crawling up in some places, and I, in an almost horizontal position on the back of my bearer, reached down and placed my hand on the ground. The greater part of the elevation of two thousand feet above the plain is made in this last climb. How cool and invigorating the air! A long pull, a strong pull, and we passed through the gateway of the stockade into the village. The people were out to give us welcome as we continued on to the farther end of the village, to the home awaiting us. There we held our first reception on the front veranda of the one mission bungalow in all those savage wilds.

Observing a generous pile of blocks and chunks of wood in the corner of the front room, used as a study, reception, and general sitting-room, I asked, "Don't you think it would be better to have the wood pile outside?" "Why, these are seats for the Nagas when they come to Sunday services or to visit us," said Mr. Clark.

The mission bungalow did not differ very materially in appearance from other houses in the village, save in size. "So big! so long! so high!" was said again and again. Certainly the hills had never witnessed anything half so grand. For sanitary reasons, the house was built on posts raised a few feet from the ground in front, and as the house site sloped quite rapidly to the rear, as Naga building lots usually do, the back of the house was fifteen to twenty feet from the ground. The walls were of crushed and platted bamboos, which in drying and shrinking produced large interstices through which not only the sun's cheerful rays peered,

Mission Bungalow—Molung

but the winds whistled as well; and not infrequently at night a lantern was the only light that would stand the breeze. In those early days the village was so small, and there was so much heavy work in house-building and clearing lands for rice growing, we were obliged to exercise much patience in waiting for many comforts which were subsequently added.

Our windows were simply openings cut in the walls, hence we were easily suited as to size and location; pieces of mat were hung outside on a smooth bamboo pole on which they could be easily drawn back and forth. There being at that time no thatch grass available for roofing, we were obliged to use the long, slender leaves of the okshi. These leaves turned on one side, and three or four of the stalks bound together made not only long, but very thick shingles, and served well to shed rain except when lifted by strong winds.

The doors of split, plaited bamboo we found very troublesome, as hung on rattan hinges they soon began to sag and scrape. Our front door was fastened by a bamboo latch on the outside. So, literally, our latch-string was always out; but the Nagas had a very annoying habit of pulling out the corner of the door at the bottom rather than lift the latch when they wished to enter. The whole house was tied together by rattans. There was not a nail in the structure.

Our heater was of the style in vogue among the people. Four sticks of timber about five inches in diameter and five or six feet long were tied together in the form

c

of a hollow square, and bound down to the floor. This space was filled with damp clay, tamped down hard, making when dry a very good hearth, whereupon blazed a cheerful fire. Our house furnishings were simple, brought up to the hill-top by Nagas, or made by them on the ground. " Why live in such a house and with so few conveniences? " has been an oft-repeated question. Anything better than the Nagas could furnish was impracticable. No builders from the plains would come into the hills. It was most unwise to expend much time or money on a building within the village stockade alongside of Naga houses of the same inflammable material. There was, at that time, no security of property or life.

Molung Village

VI

AMONG THE CLOUDS

OUR village, Molung, planted on the crest of a pro-jecting spur of the second range of hills from the plain of Assam, twenty-six hundred feet above sea level, commanded a charming view of the Brahmaputra valley. On the rolling land, beyond the extensive forests in the foreground, we could see large tea estates with their imposing bungalows and corrugated iron-roofed factories glittering in the sun. Far as the eye can reach, the early morning fogs of this valley in the cold season present a broad area of mist, rolling and tumbling like ocean billows in a storm.

Dotted over this broad expanse are native villages; miles and miles of waving grain (rice); stretches of tall grass and forest jungle, and groves of graceful, waving bamboos, all brightened by the glimmering sheen of India's greatest river, the Brahmaputra, coursing onward to the sea. Still on and beyond, passing this "son of Brahma," tower the Himalayas, their perpetual snow-capped peaks kissing the heavens in the soft, mellow light. Here is where Hindu mythology tells of a passage from earth through the ethereal dome.

Southward are seen broken ridges, mountain peak

succeeding mountain peak, hurled together in wild confusion, rising higher and still higher to ranges whence
the waters turn their course Burma-ward. How we
learned to love the soft, fleecy clouds resting quietly in
deep, dark glens, or sending their vapory sheets creep-
ing up the hillsides in charming contrast to the dark
blue mountaintops! How grandly solemn too, in a
storm!

> Not to the domes, where crumbling arch and column
>   Attest the feebleness of mortal hand,
> But to the hills, so old, so grand and solemn,
>   That God hath planned;
> Touched by a light that hath no name,
>   A glory never sung,
> Aloft on sky and mountain wall
>   Are God's great pictures hung.

In all this mountainous region the humidity of the
tropics prevails, but without the oppression of the air
of the plains. The maximum temperature during the
rains varies in different localities from seventy-eight
degrees Fahrenheit to eighty-eight degrees, and during
the cold season the minimum is from forty degrees to
fifty degrees, according to the difference in elevation.
For four months or more, successive bright, sunny
days with clear, dark blue skies give a delightful
climate.

Elevations in the immediate hills do not probably
exceed six thousand feet, while before the water-shed
is crossed between these wild tribes and " the land of

Page 37

PAPIA TREE—MOLUNG

pagodas," English government surveys record peaks of twelve thousand five hundred feet elevation.

Orchids, rhododendrons, beautifully colored begonias; the tree fern, ground fern, mosses, creepers, and vines abound in great variety and luxuriance. The hollyhock, elder, gentian, morning glory, lady slipper, blue bell, the English violet, lilies, and other homeland flowers are here found of such gigantic growth as hardly to be recognized, and one is often pleased to find himself beneath the welcome shade of the familiar oak, walnut, or other well-known trees. The Nagas give very little attention to the cultivation of fruit, but nature, as if to show the people luscious possibilities in this line, has bestowed a liberal variety of wild fruits in the jungle, such as mangoes, oranges, limes, bananas, figs, crab apples, cherries, raspberries, strawberries, and others. Few of these, however, are edible; but it is probable that most of the products of the temperate zone could be grown on the higher elevations.

The principal crop of these lands is rice; but yams, tobacco, ginger, red peppers, betel, and a limited variety of coarse vegetables are cultivated. Cotton is largely grown, from which the people weave their own cloth. Manufactures are confined mostly to cloth, simple agricultural implements, axes, spears, cooking pots, bamboo mats, baskets, etc. Tubs and pails woven of bamboo or reed are made water-tight by smearing with the juice of the rubber tree. The indigo plant is used for coloring purposes.

The soil is composed of clay in some localities, sand in others, and in many parts is exceedingly rocky; still there is much tillable land. Coal, iron, and petroleum are found in considerable quantities, but have not yet become articles of commerce; neither are they utilized by the Nagas except that in the war days petroleum— "earth oil"—was collected in bamboo tubes and thrown over the houses when the enemy desired to fire a village. There is a limited trade in rubber.

Of wild animals, the elephant and wild boar are very troublesome on the rice cultivations. When the grain is young and tender, not infrequently at dusk, a messenger will bring to the village a report that ten, fifteen, twenty or more elephants are on the rice lands. These soon make destructive work, trampling down with their huge feet more perhaps than they consume by eating. Monkeys too, in great numbers and many varieties, help themselves freely to the cultivator's subsistence. Tigers and leopards not infrequently feast on a cow, goat, or pig taken from beneath a house in the village; bears roam by night in these mountain fastnesses; wild dogs in packs and many smaller foes to domestic animals have their homes here. There is a tradition that the unicorn once roamed over these hills.

A kind of short-legged hill cattle called mithan, Bengal bison or gyall, a fine animal of the *bos frontalis* species, is common, both wild and domesticated. The latter is used only in paying off war indemnities, and for great feasts which are given by the chief men of the villages; one such feast sometimes costing, with the animal and other accessories, including floods of rice beer, five or six hundred rupees—two hundred dollars. This may call for the last rupee and not infrequently incurs a debt of long standing.

VII

NAGAS, recognizing that fever lurks in the low-lands, but more especially for protection in war, choose for their village sites the steep, rugged mountain peaks and ridges. The main approaches to the villages are exceedingly pretty, and often quite imposing. Broad, open avenues, kept clear from jungle growth, and bordered by shrubs of fine trees, among which the oak is a favorite, lead up to the massive village gates. The villagers take great pride in showing these, hoping thereby to impress strangers with their numbers, strength, and enterprise.

There were formerly outside each gateway one or two ditches, ten or twelve feet wide and six or eight feet deep, corresponding to a dry moat in English fortifications. These trenches were thickly studded with sharp bamboo spikes, and spanned by a single log, thus rendering impossible the rapid escape of enemies when attacking a village ; and when pressed into these moats quick work was made of them, and the village skull house lavishly replenished.

The villages were also strongly fortified by stockades built of sharpened posts set closely together, sometimes in double rows, and about midway to the top was a

40

cheval-de-frise with its bristling bamboo spikes turned outward, impossible to be scaled. Imposing roofs covered the village gateways, and massive wooden doors closed these entrances at night. These heavy doors turned on hinges shaped in the hewing, and in the centre of each door was a huge knob, with an orifice through which passed a big bar by which the door was fastened.

Close by the village gates, and high up in nearby trees, either within or without the stockade, lookout houses were built, and occupied by sentinels.

Within and near the gates were the " barracks " for unmarried warriors, abounding in unmistakable evidences of an uncivilized and barbarous people. On the great central post (and one might wonder how such a giant timber could be brought by hand from its home in the forest) were carved very good representations of men, elephants, tigers, leopards, all highly colored in gray, yellow, black, and red; while skins of the favorite hornbill, lizards, snakes, and skulls—human and imitation—found a place in the various decorations. The young warriors slept with their battle-axes for pillows and their spears close at hand. Extra spear shafts and large quantities of torch material were kept in readiness. On a large platform outside guards sat smoking and lazily amusing themselves throughout the day; village courts and political councils were held here.

Nearby was the enormous village drum—a hardwood tree trunk hollowed out—its larger end elaborately carved, and usually representing some animal. It could be heard for miles around. It was the tocsin of alarm to summon the people from their fields or wheresoever in case of war or fire, and was also used on festive occasions.

In addition to the " barracks " and the watch-houses there were in most villages one or more public houses or sheds, which were a rendezvous for the men when idle or engaged in braiding mats and baskets or making culinary vessels, implements of husbandry, and the like. Later these houses have been frequently used for preaching services and Sunday-schools. The missionary, when touring, sometimes made one of these houses his temporary abode.

The dwellings formerly and to this day stand close together in order to occupy the least possible space and to be the more easily defended. They are always built with the gable fronting the street, the projecting ridge pole of the large houses, particularly those of the first families, not infrequently overtopping their less pretentious neighbors across the way. On either side of the main thoroughfare in large villages, unless the slope is too precipitous, houses stand two or three tiers deep down the hillside, the elevated rear platform of one house extending over the front door of the one next below. Occasionally below the houses may be found a wee enclosure for a few vegetables, but these are not numerous, as cows, pigs, and fowls have right of way.

Vegetables are mostly grown on the rice cultivations, often miles from the village.

The houses of the more well-to-do are readily recognized by their size, and more especially their prominent bow fronts and conspicuous embellishments. Usually a cooking pot turned upside down, bound on the gable, symbolizes hospitality. Under the bow fronts are set crotched trunks of trees, memorializing heroic deeds or special feasts given to the village.

The houses are built long and narrow with steep roofs, which project in front several feet beyond the outside walls, thus forming somewhat spacious verandas, where guests are entertained. Numerous pigs, dogs, and fowls enjoy the shade, and much work is done there. The first room, answering to a front hall, extending crosswise, has an earth floor, and is furnished with a large wooden mortar for hulling rice. The pig trough is here, and here the domestic animals pass the night, although Mr. Cock and Mrs. Hen usually perch farther on in the family room. There is never a chimney. In the centre of the house is the clay hearth, in which tripods of stones set firmly furnish supports for the cooking vessels. The bright, cheerful blaze at evening lights the house, while the smoke serves in lieu of mosquito netting and also protects from sand flies. Over this fire hangs the pantry—two or three tiers of bamboo shelves suspended from the roof by strong rattans.

Hanging on pegs thrust into the walls are various

articles, and every well-to-do family has a basket with a tight-fitting cover in which valuables are kept, such as expensive jewelry and clothes for occasional or holiday wear. The nest of the setting hen also finds its peg on the wall.

Near the fire stand the bedsteads, which are also utilized for seats during the day. For strangers or an unusual number of friends there are always spare blocks of wood at hand. The bedsteads may be only a few bamboos placed closely on a frame or a solid plank with legs and pillow formed in the hewing. These are the favorite styles, and anything soft seems never to have been thought of, even for the sick. On one occasion when there was an alarm of fire a young man, seriously ill, was brought into the mission bungalow, laid upon a mattress and given a pillow. Recovering a little from the shock the poor fellow exclaimed, " So soft! so soft! " while his attendants declared that such ease would " break " their sleep.

The people are very social, gathering in little groups in the street under the projecting roofs in front of their houses or on the rear platform. Rows of women, each hunting pigmy foes in the hair of the one immediately in front of her, is a familiar sight.

VIII

SAVAGE ORATORY AND VISITING CARDS

THE Nagas, once civilized and Christianized, will make a manly, worthy people. In stature they are medium and in color not so dark as the natives of Bengal or Africa. Ethnologically, they may be denominated Indo-Chinese or Tibeto-Burman. Their language shows considerable mental capacity.

Each village is a little democracy managing its own affairs, except as other villages interfere either voluntarily or by partisan invitation; each has its head men, called tartars, who are the civil magistrates. These may hold office for a limited term of years or for life, or may be set aside by the village for unworthiness, unpopularity, or bad administration. They have entire control of civil matters, look after the entertainment of distinguished guests and of persons coming on official errands, and have power to impress the service of the village for any labor necessary to the well-being of the community. They have no salaries, but are well paid in perquisites and gratuitous labor. All higher offices, civil, military, and priestly, are held by those of mature years, the younger men not objecting to this, as each one hopes that in due time his turn will come.

At inter-village councils the speakers exhibit consid-

erable oratorical power, and but one is allowed to speak
at a time. Arranging his gay blanket in a flowing,
graceful style over the right shoulder, he has free use of
his arm for gesticulation, and improves the opportunity
without stint or hindrance. In his right hand he holds
his spear, and at the close of an important statement
gives emphasis by thrusting it into the ground in front
of him.

A casual observer would never imagine the ambition
for fame and glory that lurks even to this day in the
Naga's breast. He is ready to sacrifice to the utmost
that his praises may be sung and his name perpetuated.
The highest type of glory of which he formerly had any
conception was bravery and success in war. Village
sites were chosen, planned, and built with reference
to war, and paths were kept to the mountain ridges and
highlands in order to avoid giving advantage to skulk-
ing foes. Travelers went in large companies, and men,
while at work on the cultivation of their fields, stacked
their spears and shields near at hand. Guards and sentinels were everywhere. Women and children in
groups brought wood from the jungles and water from
the springs far down the hillsides, never going singly,
as the lower springs were favorite lurking places for
enemies seeking human heads. Mothers, on leaving
for their work, charged the older children, on the first
alarm of war, to seize the little ones and flee at once to
some hiding place in the jungle.

Nagas have told us when war waged hottest they

VILLAGE GATEWAY—NAGAS GOING TO THEIR WORK

did not even straighten themselves out at full length
at night, but with battle-axes under their heads and
spears at hand they lay with knees bent ready to spring
to action. The heads of women and children counted
as much as those of men, the long black hair of women
being especially prized for decorations. It was not
uncommon for a company of young men to bind themselves with an oath to refrain from the gratification of
some coveted pleasure until they had brought the head
of an enemy into the village. Such trophies won the
privilege of ornamenting spear shafts and battle-axe
handles with tufts of hair, black or dyed red and yellow, adorning their blankets with cowrie shells, and
wearing boar-tusk necklaces. Men were dubbed
women or cows until they had contributed to the village skull-house. Young maidens instigated their
betrothed to this bloody work, and it was woman's
voice that trilled the cry of victory when these prizes
reeking in blood were brought into the village.

On asking the population of a village the number of
its warriors was given. The " visiting cards " of our
guests in those days were brightly decorated spears,
and each morning on my return from school the number of callers was quickly determined by counting the
spears standing in front of the door; thus too the men
at our Sunday services were numbered.

The rice lands of two friendly villages were adjoining. Ungma was much larger than its neighbor, Sungdia, but the latter enjoyed a far-famed war record. The

people of both villages were working their lands at the same time, when the Sungdia young women began chanting war songs, and with much braggadocio called out contemptuously to Ungma workers: "Oh, you are a great people, your village is large and your lands spread over much territory, and yet you dare not attack us, a little community, but too plucky for you; oh, shame! shame! you big Ungma." At this Ungma's young bloods were fired, and rushing unsuspectingly upon the Sungdias a head was taken, whereupon one of the biggest wars of the tribe was opened, which cost Ungma several hundred cattle and many pigs.

Previous to annexation to British rule slavery existed universally throughout the Ao tribe. The slaves were frequently given to pay off war indemnities, and the harboring of fugitives often resulted in war.

IX

THE SAVAGE IN COSTUME AND AT WORK

THERE is no degradation of women among the Nagas. Although not sharing directly in civil or military administration, yet in both of these they exert a strong, subtle influence, and emulate the lover's and husband's pride in war medals. Girls are usually betrothed from the age of eleven to fourteen years, parents generally arranging for this union, but the young people sometimes make their own choice. During the interval between engagement and marriage the young man makes himself very useful in the family of his betrothed, and when successful in fishing or the chase shares his booty with the anticipated parents-in-law, which attention announces the engagement, while the accepted lover keeps close guard over his girl, as his title *aninuker* (girl-watcher) implies. Either party proving false, the parents of the offender are fined, often to the extent of several cows or pigs; but in case of poverty, spears and rice are the penalty.

Marriage is celebrated by the bridegroom simply taking his bride to a new home, but in well-to-do families a feast is served and wedding presents bestowed. The bride's family furnishes the larger part of the necessary " setting out," consisting of one or

D

more new cloths for the daughter, a new sleeping mat, a wooden plate, a drinking mug, a winnowing tray, harvest baskets, and bamboo water vessels. These, with the bedstead and implements of husbandry, which the groom supplies, are considered a generous house furnishing. Remarriage in less than two or three years after the death of a husband or wife is not considered good form.

Polygamy is not practised, and separations are uncommon. Divorces may be obtained from the village court, or there may be a mutual separation. The usual cause of divorce is adultery, but failure on the part of the wife to become a mother is considered a justifiable reason for parting. Nagas are very fond of their children and depend much upon them for support in declining years.

Housekeeping in these simple homes is easy. Each member of the family, taking his bark or wooden dish, helps himself, and when he has eaten, turns down his dish on the shelf suspended over the hearth. Dishwashing is optional. "Tom and Dick" are unacquainted with bread, pies, and cake; pickling and preserving days are unknown. Does one wish a lunch to take to the cultivation or the chase, some cold rice with a little relish of dried fish, bits of dried meat, and red peppers are tied in a leaf, and he is off. Infrequent ablutions are performed at springs or in streams. A towel in the form of a rattan or bamboo splint scrapes the water off and nature finishes the drying.

TRADING IN PIGS

The boys wear their birthday suits with the occasional blankets until they are pretty well grown, hence there are no trousers out at the knees or coats at the elbows. The little sisters are clothed earlier, but with no ruffles or frills to tax strength and patience. The parents and little ones go to bed by the light of a bright, cheerful fire on the open hearth. The boys, as soon as old enough, go to the barracks to sleep, and the older girls collect at the homes of widows. The people get up in the morning with their bedding on—the blanket worn optionally during the day. For guests the spare bed is the best mat in the house.

But there is real work for the women. While men do the heaviest part of the cultivation, they share in preparing the land, seed sowing, weeding, and harvesting the crops. And after the grain is gathered, before it is ready to feed a large family, much time and strength are required. First, the paddy—unhulled rice—must be dried in the sun, and while spread out on a mat a small boy or girl, an old aunty or aged grandmother, armed with a long pole, keeps watch for chickens, pigs, and goats. Then follows the pounding in a large wooden mortar, the chaff being separated by tossing all on a bamboo tray. The life of the Naga woman is hard—hard from the character of much of her work, but worse from exposure in all kinds of weather, sparse clothing, and poor diet. They gin the cotton by laying it across a smooth stone and pressing out the seeds with a hand roller, but among the border villages the simple machine of the Assamese for this work is fast being introduced. Spinning is done by pulling out the roll and twisting thread under the palm of the hand over the bare knee, at the same time running it onto a spindle held in the right hand. The shuttles fly swiftly through the little bamboo looms, usually fastened to the front of the house outside, a favorite place for a tête-à-tête and much gossip.

The full dress of a woman, if we except her ornaments, consists of a heavy cotton cloth in form of a towel extending from just above the hips down to the knee. The color is indigo blue, striped with fine red lines. For the more stylish there are woven into the cloth figures in dog's hair plucked from the living animal and dyed red.

Every person, old or young, has a cotton blanket, dirty white or indigo blue. The cloths of the wealthy may be gaily colored and ornamented with shells. The blanket is always worn by young women drawn around the body close underneath the arms, and covering the chest until motherhood. To this sparse costume is added a profusion of ornaments. Through the upper rim of each ear of the women is worn a triple-coiled brass ring about nine inches in circumference, held upright against the head by a cord joining ring to ring. Through the lobe of the ears hang thick pieces of glass or quartz crystals about two inches square. Close about the throat are the " diamonds and pearls " in the form of pointed shells strung with carnelian beads, a

WOMEN AT THE LOOMS

pretty adornment to these dark skins. Then follow many strings of beads of varying sizes, which, with a heavy brass chain, reach very nearly or quite to the waist line. Heavy brass bracelets encircle the wrists.

Every Naga woman who is not sold into slavery when young has a pair of indigo blue striped stockings, which last a lifetime, tattooed in the skin. On the chin are also tattooed vertical lines, widening and deepening as they extend down on the neck, and in many instances crossing the chest in elongated diamond shape. This very painful operation of tattooing is patiently submitted to by the girls when twelve or fourteen years of age. The diet of the women, always meagre, is further limited after the tattooing. Very few women eat flesh, except fish, and none use eggs or milk. Their food is largely rice and coarse vegetables. All drink rice beer.

Men wear merely a girdle about the loins, with a small apron. Those who can afford it ornament this cloth by figures in brightly colored dog's hair. The block of wood in which rests the axe, worn on the back of every man and boy, may well be considered a part of the dress. The men are not, however, without their jewelry. Large tufts of white, fluffy cotton are drawn through apertures in the ear; cotton is also made into compact balls and fastened just in front of the ear. Long brass tubes with chains attached, also tassels of brightly colored hair, are used as ear ornaments. Necklaces of wild boar tusks, ivory armlets of elephant tusks, and bracelets of cowrie shells contribute to the warrior's pride. Those who have taken human heads may also decorate their scant cloths with cowrie shells. On great occasions there are also added rattan helmets, fantastically trimmed with boar tusks, plumes of goat hair, tufts of hog's bristles, and the long tail feathers of the hornbill, the bird of victory. Hair cutting is done by lifting the hair over an axe and striking down upon it with a hard mallet. Men, women, and children smoke tobacco of their own raising in pipes mostly of common bamboo, while some of the better class aspire to an iron pipe skilfully manufactured by their own smiths. Babes in arms play with their mothers' pipes, thus early becoming accustomed to the use of the weed.

Amid these exhibitions of taste so degrading and repulsive we observe with encouragement and delight the slightest evidence of some innate refinement. Men as well as women and children are often seen coming from the jungle or from the day's work with pretty, delicate wild flowers, or even a twig of fresh green drawn through the orifice in the ear. Our own villagers and strangers too often come asking for flowers from our garden. The Assamese costume of jacket and body cloth is now being adopted by many who have come under Christian influence, especially the pupils in the schools, but the habits of the older ones are still as the laws of the Medes and Persians.

The harvest is a time both of hard work and much merriment. Pigs carried squealing to the harvest field

MAKING BASKETS, DRINKING-CUPS, DISHES, ETC.

re familiar sights and sounds during these busy days. n the cold season there is house building, making and epairing bedsteads, dishes, pig troughs, mats, and askets. Bundles and bundles of rattan—the Naga's ails and strings—are the work of odd jobs. This is lso the time for travel, trade, and war. In the baskets f the long procession of traders en route to Assam are runting pigs and squawking fowls to be disposed of here, and rolls of nice new mats to be quickly picked p by Europeans and natives in the plains. In the askets so securely bound over with fresh palm leaves re ginger root, red peppers, and bundles of betel leaf or chewing. These same palm leaves, the Naga's 'green silk umbrellas," serve in chance showers to over the salt brought up in exchange for articles sold.

The bright cold-season days are frequently enlivened too by hunting and fishing, but the great civil event is the dress parade, when the military march through the main village streets and on an open space at either end of the village go through their drill, dance, and perform many feats of athletics. Dressed in the gayest colored cloths, caps of bear skins and of bamboo splints decorated with feathers, quills, boar tusks, tufts, and tassels of bamboo shavings and monkey tails, their appearance is most fantastic. Spears and battle-axes, brightened for the occasion and glittering in the sun, and newly decorated war shields add much to the picturesqueness of the scene.

The Nagas, although a busy, hard-working people

(the average annual income of a family is probably not more than twenty or thirty dollars), subject to privation, exposure, and pestilence, are not generally melancholy or morose, rather the reverse. Even their village sacrificial offerings are seasons of more or less merriment, and at their springtime and after-harvest feasts the blood of bulls and goats flows freely and the supply of rice beer is unlimited.

VILLAGE BARBER

X

SAVAGE WORSHIP AND STRANGE LEGENDS

RELIGIOUSLY, these hill people south of Assam, not being grounded in the old systematized religions of the East, and having no caste, are far more ready to accept the simple story of Jesus of Nazareth. They believe that the soul does not die with the body, trust in omens of all sorts, and consult them in every important undertaking. All their ills are attributed to spiritual agencies; diseases, accidents, sores, and the like requiring sacrifices of fowls, pigs, or cows. The sun and moon are regarded as deities, and are occasionally worshiped, as are also the spirits of officials and ancestors. The three important deities in the Naga creed are Lungkeezingba, Mozing, and Leezaba. Lungkeezingba, the chief deity, is the god of destiny and is worshiped by the household. Mozing is the king of the spirits of the deceased; he is said to have been once a man and to have contended with another as to the chief rulership, failing in which he retired into the interior of the world, where he now presides over the realm of the dead. All departed spirits must pass to his judgment seat, where by certain tests their characters are determined and their future state assigned. Leezaba, although not the creator of the world, is said to have had a part in molding and fashioning it to its present shape. As not many of the Aos have traveled beyond their own country, their horizon embraces for them the world. Tradition has it that while Leezaba was busy with this world-shaping work, having the valley of Assam nicely leveled and finished to his satisfaction, he was about to commence reducing the hills to the same fine condition when a cockroach appeared bringing him word that war had broken out, whereupon he immediately left his work and never resumed it, hence the rough, mountainous, apparently unfinished Naga country.

Leezaba is an important deity in the Ao village worship. He has power to give good crops or to withhold the rain and the sunshine; power to send famine, disease, pestilence, and war; power to permit or cause accidents, small and great. A certain time each year he is propitiated by the village in a body in order to avert the above-mentioned ills. At this time no work is allowed, not even the pounding and hulling of the daily rice, and no one is permitted to be absent from the village, lest the whole sacrifice and service be rejected. The priests keep themselves in seclusion and ceremonially clean for six days, and each family must offer an egg on its own cultivation. The Aos attribute a spiritual existence and supernatural power to all their deities. Certain rocks and pools are regarded as their abode, and are reverently and cautiously passed.

On one of the frequent marches between Molung

POUNDING RICE

and Dekha Haimong villages, Mr. Clark inquired why
the path at a certain point made such a sudden detour
down the steep hillside. He was told that an enormous
rock, standing vertically and alone and in which dwelt
a mighty and influential spirit, was up there, and no
one must pass that way. Mr. Clark kept to the ridge,
and to the amazement of his attendants walked back
and forth unharmed before the sacred boulder. This
direct and easy route, close to his lordship's stony
abode, was gradually more and more ventured upon,
and ere long well cleared and opened as a public highway. It was, however, some time before women ventured on the path, but the old-time road has now long
since grown up to jungle, and all sorts of desecrations
are practised on that once hallowed stone by boys who
have outgrown their fathers' theology.

The Aos define sin as " unclean," " foul," " a stain,"
" a spot," and greatly abhor anything they denominate
sin. They live in great dread and fear of it, and cleans-
ing from sin is costly both in sacrifices and time.
When a woman dies in childbirth all her jewelry, much
as it is prized and expensive as it may be, must all be
thrown away to be rooted over by pigs and destroyed.
The death of any one caused by falling from a tree or
any height, by a snake bite, or by a wild animal, is evidence of sin. For this last sin the seclusion of the entire village is demanded for six days, while the family
in which such violent death has occurred must immediately forsake their own house and everything in it,

living in little huts built on the outskirts of the village, changing every few days from one hut to another, and keeping themselves entirely aloof from others. In the meantime some aged friend supplies their necessities, but must not speak to them. This continues until the next new moon, when the unfortunate family, **fur-nished** with clothing by relatives, leave what they have worn while in disgrace, and now, regarded as purified, emerge from their ostracism. No property remains to the unfortunate ones but real estate; their house may have been ever so good, it is now left to decay, and if they have crops growing they must not be harvested. If there are betel palm gardens (this leaf is much culti-vated and sold in the plains for chewing and is a profit-able source of income), the leaf must not be plucked for one year. Atonement for sin among the Aos costs something, and no strong argument is required to con-vince them of personal sin and the need of salvation therefrom.

When Molung village was still small and quite sur-rounded by jungle, a woman coming up from her day's work on the cultivation was carried off by a tiger. The alarm was quickly brought to the village and there was a general stampede for the search, but increasing dark-ness soon compelled a fruitless return. At peep of day every able-bodied man of the village was ready for a tiger hunt. On finding the remains of the woman, Mr. Clark was besought to inject poison therein, and soon the much dreaded foe was found stretched lifeless where he had taken his last meal. The animal was borne to the village in triumph and placed on an elevated platform; and the shouts of rejoicing that went up would make the American " three cheers " sound in comparison like a drawing-room solo. The tiger's skin decorated the bamboo floor of our Naga drawing-room.

In this incident there came to this new and nominally Christian village a test of sincerity, faithfulness, and courage in abandoning old-time superstitions. The village was " bound," and for three days the people sat in council, while we waited with deep interest and in earnest prayer the decision. We are happy to record that Christianity triumphed. In order to prove the honesty of their convictions, the whole village was rallied to work on the cultivation of the afflicted family, which would have been a most dreadful venture under the old conditions. It is considered an omen of ill to be the first to enter a village where a person has been suddenly killed, and no stranger will knowingly do this for one week after such a calamity. On the occasion mentioned, an embassy on important business was en route to our village, and immediately turned back on learning of the terrible event.

From the abundant folk-lore of the Aos the following came to us; its source can hardly be conjectured. Two brothers went fishing, and, successful in their catch, cut for a cooking pot a section of bamboo, thrust into it while yet alive a good, plump specimen of their game, added water, placed a crumpled leaf in the open end of the bamboo for a stopple, and, putting the vessel over the fire, sat down to await their repast. On turning out the fish when it was supposed to be cooked, imagine their consternation on seeing the creature flopping about fish-fashion, evidently unharmed! What! wouldn't boiling a fish kill it? Returning the fish to the bamboo, a leaf from another tree was utilized for a stopple, when in due time the fish was cooked. The brothers consulted together, and were so curious to know if there could be any virtue in the leaf stopple that they resolved, after carefully examining the first leaf, to try another from the same tree, whereupon the fish was restored to life. If there is actually a leaf which will give perpetual life to animals, why not to man? the brothers reasoned. They very carefully noted the kind of tree, and agreed between themselves to keep the knowledge a close secret. Subsequently, if a member of either family were ill, leaves from this particular tree were placed under the head, and the sick invariably recovered. These families increased and were fast becoming the dominant power in the village. They grew haughty, overbearing, and insolent, until those not in the secret could endure them no longer, and a plot was laid to annihilate them and their now numerous progeny. All were destroyed save one small boy who knew not the leaves for healing; hence a knowledge of a tree of life perished from among the Aos.

In directing our attention to a certain prominent

mountain peak, the people have told us that in the sub-
merging of the whole world ages ago this elevation
alone remained above the surging waters. Have these
ignorant people some tradition of the true flood?

Again, Mr. Clark, in his Bible translation, has had
no difficulty in finding an Ao word for " the fire that
never shall be quenched." The idea too is advanced
that in the last days men will be filled with all manner
of wickedness, and that everything will be consumed
in a great world conflagration.

They also have a tradition that in the earliest period
after creation man and all animate beings lived in
peace, and that in the last days man will become very
degenerate and all on earth will be consumed.

XI

GOD'S ACRE AMONG THE AOS

SEEZING, the richest man in Molung village, died. His property was largely in lands covered with betel-nut palms and pepper vines, in cows and pigs, war accouterments and ornaments, with a fine house and more than the requisite amount of furnishings. He was a man of unusual intelligence and had a good, kind face. He never professed Christianity, but was a frequent attendant upon religious services, and always respectful to the missionary and his teachings. Early in his illness he sent for Mr. Clark to administer medicine. The disease not yielding readily, and the family becoming alarmed, preparations were made for propitiatory offerings to the spirits. Christians pleaded with the family, and warned them against offending the one Great Spirit, yet the wife was unrelenting. A pig was slain, then a cow, but the disease still raged; five pigs and a dog were offered, but to no avail. Messengers were despatched to a distant village to consult a renowned soothsayer. Other animals were called for by the diviner, but before this last demand reached the home of the sick man another messenger was claiming its victim. The poor penitent called for the missionary, but alas, too late! The soul had gone out in

64

darkness. At once a dog was slain that its spirit might accompany the dead on its journey to the unknown. The same evening a pig was killed initiatory to the great feast to follow on the morrow, and the devoted wife continued all night to chant the praises of her husband. The following days several more pigs were killed to feast relatives and friends who gathered to commemorate the virtues of the departed.

For several succeeding days, fantastically arranged in front of the late residence of the dead, were all his household possessions, and his war regalia, conspicuous among which was the shield of buffalo hide embellished with grotesque figures in white paint made of the calcined skulls of pigs. His personal ornaments were also on exhibition, while skulls, real and imitation, numbered his human victims. Skulls of cows and pigs and long rows of bamboo water vessels, symbolical of rice beer, represented his many and generous feasts to the village.

The body of Seezing, by his own request, was dried in smoke before being deposited in its last resting-place —a not infrequent occurrence among the Nagas. For this process the body is suspended over a fire in the front entrance of the house or in the living-room, and remains thus for weeks, months, and, in rare instances, for a year.

Just across the way, in striking contrast with the above, there lay in a Christian home the silent form of a much-loved child. A few flowers placed at the

E

head seemed especially, in this time of dense darkness, to shed a ray of light and a gleam of hope. As we tried to offer sympathy to the sorrowing ones the Christian father replied, " It is our heavenly Father who has taken from us our precious child." We gathered a little band of His children in that rude Naga hut, not so spacious and grand as the former, but where the blessed word was read, prayer offered, and the Spirit's presence gave peace and comfort.

The Nagas usually set up a terrible wail over their dead, shrieking and howling long and loud that the gods may be assured the loss is sufficiently appreciated. These sounds borne to us, frequently on the stillness of the night air, have been indeed sad and heartrending.

When bodies are not dried, relatives and friends gather material and prepare the coffins. These are miniature houses, almost a facsimile of their own dwellings, and much artistic taste and skill is displayed in their construction. They are just large enough to receive the body; are tightly closed and borne away, amid the long-continued wails and lamentations of the family; then are placed on a platform, five or six feet above the ground, and covered by a roof, sometimes enclosed by walls. In the front of this shed or rude house are hung the cloths and ornaments of the dead, also the honored and much-coveted human skulls, habiliments of war, baskets, mats, and often rows of bamboo vessels, supposed to contain rice beer for the soul on its journey. The ground close around is stuck with sharp bamboo spikes as protection against the ravages of wild beasts. The cemeteries are located just outside the village on the main path, and by their decorations ofttimes present a grotesque appearance.

From the establishment of our Molung village, skulls as decorations were not permitted in its cemetery. One day a man brought in eight human skulls strung on a bamboo pole. A stranger had died in Molung, and his friends were bringing these wherewith to dignify his last resting-place, but they were not allowed. For sanitary reasons, and for the better protection of the body from ravages of wild animals, Christians and many others are now burying their dead.

XII

EVERYDAY LIFE AT MOLUNG

BRINGING the gospel to these savage hill tribes · taxed to the utmost the resources of the missionary. A good knowledge of their language, habits, and character is absolutely essential for gaining their confidence and winning souls. Some knowledge of medicine also is of great advantage; it is an open door into many homes, and puts an end to consulting soothsayers and sacrificing to demons. Medical works were therefore added to our library. Frequent councils were held with our people on village and inter-village matters; ambassadors from beyond our borders came for advice, and thus many difficulties were settled in a satisfactory and peaceable manner which otherwise might have ended in bloody conflict. We were ever alert to show the people that we were not among them for the benefit of a single village, but for the best good of all.

In our visits to these rude homes we were always well received. It was often difficult to climb over the high front door-sills when Mrs. Swine and her family were blocking the entrance, but, once inside, the softest block of wood the house afforded was offered us, and in gratitude for our call we were frequently urged to accept a few red peppers, a squash, or other vegetables.

68

On one occasion a woman, anxious to express her appreciation of help received during her illness, drew from underneath a hen, setting in a basket hanging from the wall, two glossy eggs, saying, "Here, Mem Sahib, take these; I don't know why they don't hatch."

Many are the poor, emaciated ones in these rude homes, tossing with pain, lying on bare planks, with only threadbare cloths about them. There may be seen a woman in terrible pain, propped up in a reclining position by blocks of wood; another affectionately supported by her strong, burly husband, and mothers nursing children sick with bowel trouble, while at the same time giving them green corn or cucumbers.

The people of our village were, in their way, considerate of us, and evidently tried to show us sympathy in our isolation; and yet, poor creatures, how could they appreciate what we were giving up to bring so much to them! A Naga, returning from work one day, came up to us holding by the tail a huge lizard, and asked, "Father, will you eat a piece?" Perhaps we looked hungry.

"What ye shall eat" was ever with us a question. The skinny fowls, scavengers of the village, were not always to be had, while beefsteak and mutton chops were strangers to our board save as they rarely appeared in the form of venison, wild pig, or goat meat. Eggs were scarce, and as Nagas do not milk their cows, we were deprived of this luxury, while vegetables that we could utilize were rare; thus we were early driven to add the care of farm and garden to our labors. Our " corner grocery " was Calcutta, one thousand miles away, our necessities coming by steamer up the Bramaputra river to the mouth of the Jhanzi, thence by native boats to Amguri Tea Garden, and from there on natives' backs to our hilltop.

One night tigers took three of our cows and several goats, and some smaller foe robbed us of four kids. By poisoning the remains of the cows, the second feast of their tiger majesties gave us two beautifully marked skins. Through this loss of milk, the butter on our bread was thin, and sometimes wanting altogether, as our tinned supply was largely consumed, and our far-away grocery required two months in filling orders.

The difficulty of getting up our supplies in the rains made it necessary to stock our larder in March to last till the following November, and from every lack we must learn a lesson by which to profit for our next season's order. In that humid atmosphere our food supplies, though carefully sealed, often became mouldy and not infrequently very much alive, requiring sunnings and siftings.

Ignorance of Anglo-Indian terms sometimes occasioned amusing disappointments in filling our Calcutta orders. For milk-pans came preserving kettles, and tins for baking bread melted at the first heating. " What are these? " exclaimed a neighbor missionary as he drew forth from the box he was unpacking two long

strips of steel, each just one yard in length, " I didn't
order these." " One pair of steelyards " read the order,
and not the " balance " of British vernacular.

One of our greatest privations was our slow and uncertain mail. Our nearest postal delivery was Amguri,
fifteen miles distant, reached only by the fording of two
rivers, which in the rainy season were swollen beyond
the Nagas' depth; consequently two or three weeks,
and occasionally a month or more, passed without any
communication outside our own dark parish. But when
our mails did come, can words express our joy, how we
in turn laughed and wept over the precious letters from
the home land! After one of these mail famines we
started off our accumulated pile of letters and clothes
for laundering. What was our dismay when at night-
fall our carriers appeared empty-handed. On their return journey they bravely waded into the strong and
rapid current of the swollen Jhanzi, but, soon finding
themselves beyond their depth and unable to swim,
they cast aside every weight, and thus our anticipated
mail and fresh laundry went floating on and on, for
aught we know, to the sea.

On another occasion our carriers left Amguri late in
the afternoon, but before the dense forest of the low-
lands was passed two elephants charged down upon
them. Surprised and greatly frightened, not even stopping to grasp their spears, they scampered as quickly
as possible up the nearest tree. The elephants upset
their baskets, and not finding salt or anything they

cared for, began trumpeting, stamping, and tearing up the ground. Unable to shake down from the tree its human tenants, the elephants waited and watched until dawn, when the female sloped off with her young, and her disgusted mate soon followed.

There was difficulty in early persuading the women that this new religion was for them as well as for their husbands and sons, and thus they were a decided hindrance to the extension of Christianity in the village. It was with great difficulty that a Christian man with an unconverted wife could prevent sacrifices and offerings for the restoration of the sick. There would come the taunt, "Oh, you don't care if we die. You are not willing to give anything to save us. You have taken the Sahib's religion, and do not care longer for your family."

Awaking one morning and hearing Mr. Clark in earnest conversation with a caller, I soon recognized that the trouble was concerning the old "Leezaba worship." The man was a professing Christian, conscientious and faithful, yet in his ignorance and great agitation of mind was seeking wisdom. His wife, very ill, was growing worse; and her relatives, rushing into the house, demanded a sacrifice for the demons. "I do not believe in it," the man was saying, "but what shall I— what can I do?" After conference and prayer the man left the house saying, "Well, I'll not sacrifice; I'll not sacrifice, and I'll go back and tell the family so." He did it. Prayers were heard, and the wife recovered.

A terrific gale visited us one night just at the opening of the rains. We had scarcely known anything so severe before. Awakened by the creaking of the bed and the shaking of the house, we arose, but from the unsteadiness of the house could scarcely walk. Continuous flashes of lightning glared through the roofing, lifted by the wind. It seemed certain that the house must go. I exclaimed, " Let us get out, go into a Naga hut, somewhere nearer the ground " (our house was raised on high posts). Mr. Clark replied, " Why, you cannot stand on the hill." We soon found a place of safety, and it was awfully sublime to listen to the roaring of the winds, sweeping from mountain peak to mountain peak, as they welled up through the grand old forest, and burst in wrathful fury over our unprotected hilltop. But He who commands the winds and the waves had said, " Hitherto." The next morning found us not exactly in ruins, but in such a plight! The village head men came to inquire after us, and the service of the village was placed at our disposal.

Foggy, lonely days, there were at times; weeks and weeks of these in the long season of drizzling rain and drifting fog, driving through our mat walls, when our open fire on the hearth failed to keep us dry. " Oh, the mould! how it gathers on the walls! would it were only on the walls! " wrote Emily Judson. But sunshine followed, walls dried, carriers went for the mails, and all was well again.

For a little change of scene a trip to our nearest

village was decided upon. A ticket for the outing, in the form of three men for my chair, was secured, and we started, accompanied by a goodly number of our people. Arriving at the village we were very hospitably entertained at the home of one of the "first families." Rice beer and a leaf for chewing being offered us and refused, our hostess asked, "Well, what do you eat and drink?" A bystander suggesting sugar cane, it was quickly brought, which out of politeness we accepted. So pleased were the people with our visit that the killing of a pig for a feast was proposed. This, of course, was not permitted. They urged us to spend the night, promising comfortable quarters, a fowl, eggs, and vegetables. Declining this invitation, it was insisted that we must, at least, take a fowl home with us. On our return fifteen men from distant Merangkong village were awaiting an interview.

Not infrequently there came change and variety of a different character—changes unsought. I quote from my journal: "Just at evening, coming up through the village gate and passing our bungalow, were twenty-four men dressed in all the habiliments of war, bamboo splint hats trimmed with wild boar tusks, the red band, an unmistakable insignia of bloody deeds, battle-axes, spears, and shields highly embellished, and the feathers of their favorite bird indicative of victory. As their coming had been heralded by the previous arrival of messengers, there was no special alarm. Although professing friendship, it was contrary to custom to enter a friendly village with all this paraphernalia of war. The authorities ordered the men disarmed. They stoutly objected, but the command was peremptory; so arms were stacked in front of our veranda, which now presented its gayest appearance. The following morning twenty more men of this party arrived; being slow to make known their business they were zealously watched, and it was soon learned that they were really on the war-path and had come to consult a renowned soothsayer, now stopping in Molung."

As further illustration of life in this land of war, I cite another instance. While taking one day our five o'clock tea, suddenly we heard screams from women and children; saw mothers hurrying with their little ones in arms and dragging others after them, and boys and girls running past our window helter-skelter down the hillside toward the jungle. Our servant exclaimed, "There is war, Mem Sahib, there is war!" and, as if in the same breath, the alarm was sounded throughout the village. We were now thoroughly aroused. Mr. Clark went to the door; there was great excitement in the village, people running to and fro. I put on my hat and began making hasty preparations for a night and more, if need be, in the jungle. But before we got off messengers from the village hastened to inform us that all was well. Warriors from another village friendly to Molung, returning from the conflict dressed in their war regalia, had unceremoniously entered within our gates; the women and children seeing them were frightened, hence gave the alarm which others quickly caught up, and there was confusion and commotion on all sides. In the meantime the strange guests added to the fright by running hither and thither, trying to assure the people that they were friends and that no hostility was contemplated. They were, however, severely reprimanded by the village authorities.

In these early days among the Nagas, alarms like the above were of no uncommon occurrence. Molung was weak in able-bodied men—warriors; hence every one was on the alert, watchful and suspicious. It was not uncommon that weaker villages were ravaged by the stronger, simply for heads. Every night there were guards at our gateways and exposed points about the village; and there were always some men detained in the village during the day. There was kept on our bamboo bedpost a bag containing certain valuable articles which could be picked up quickly in the emergency of a hasty flight; this bag also contained bits of cloth and paper to strew along my way, in order that I might be traced, in case of separation from others.

There came messengers from brave and warlike Sungdia, unable to combat with smallpox which had broken out there and in neighboring villages. The Nagas have great dread of this disease, and when it rages badly their only remedy is temporarily to abandon the village and scatter, two or three families living together here and there in the jungle until the epidemic is stayed. These Sungdia men asked that Godhula

might go and do for them what had so successfully been accomplished in Merangkong village under
like circumstances. We happened to have a good quan-
tity of fresh lymph, recently furnished us by an English civil surgeon. The circumstances were made
known to Godhula and the decision left entirely with
him. To reach Sungdia village was a three days' jour-,
ney, and much of the way through a war country; he
would also be at the mercy of warriors during his entire absence. But, appreciating this opportunity of
making known the message of eternal life, Godhula
quickly replied, " Sahib, give me the lymph and I will
go." The disease was controlled in a great measure,
the village became our friends, and the gospel was
preached to the people.

It is not necessary to refer to my journal to recall
experiences of severe illness at the mission bungalow,
with no physician near.

After our first nine months' sojourn in our own parish without having seen a white face, we made a brief
visit to our old first mission home, Sibsagor. How
we did enjoy a little touch again with civilization; fel-
lowship with our missionary and English friends, Assamese Christians, and even the warm greetings of our
heathen neighbors were very pleasant. Arranging to
return by bullock cart and elephant, Colonel Campbell
very kindly asked, " Why not go via the tea gardens?
It is a little farther, but so much pleasanter. I'll send
you by pony trap to Nazira; the superintendent of the

Assam Tea Company will help you to Hati Poti garden; Hati Poti will see you to Deo Pani; and Deo Pani will land you at Amguri; you will find friends and good accommodations all the way." We did, and most appreciative and thankful we were for all. At Amguri my hill-chair awaited me and we were in due time again on the hilltop. Such a hearty welcome back from the people! One of our parishioners exclaimed, "There has been no flavor in my food since the Sahib and Mem Sahib have been away."

Later, Mr. Clark was invited to meet at Amguri the Viceroy of India on a tour through Assam, for an interview in the interest of the hill tribes. To return the same day involved a thirty-mile walk which terminated at midnight and after many difficulties. The night was fearfully dark and their path was lighted only by the ignis fatuus which was bound on the sheath of each man's battleaxe; the procession thus in Indian file, each forward man became a light to his follower.

XIII

AN ELEPHANT HUNT

IN the early days of Molung village, while the jungle grew close up around the houses and the wild inhabitants of the forest had scarcely realized our invasion of their territory, just at dusk one evening, some boys were coming up from the village grocery (a bamboo grove) with their baskets filled with luscious, young bamboo sprouts which, when pounded into pulp, constitute the Nagas' saccharine material. The hindmost boy felt something pulling and tugging at his basket; and looking back spied an elephant, " trunking " his sweets. Dropping his load he sped to the village and gave the alarm. The people were just coming in from their work, and it was too late for the chase that night; but the blood of these nimrods was stirred, and they would not sleep until they had exacted a promise from Mr. Clark to join them with his gun in the hunt on the morrow. " It is very dangerous, father," they said, " for an elephant to be thus wandering at will about the village. He is probably a ' rogue elephant ' (a solitary, maddened one). Why, our women and children will not dare venture outside after firewood or water, and what will then be left of our ripening grain? Then too, we are so hungry, father, we have been so long, you know, without meat, and here will be such a haul."

Very early the next morning the hunters were at our door. They soon struck the huge footprints of their game and traced his long route by the broken and bent shrubs, bamboos, and tall jungle grass through which his monstrous body had made a path. The sun was sinking low in the west, when, hark! a crushing and crunching among the bamboos was heard; slowly and stealthily the hunters advanced. Hush, sh-h! sh-h! on, on, quietly and cautiously. Bang! and by one well-directed shot this mass of living flesh fell to the ground. The forest rang with shouts and yells.

It was already dusk and the hunters were alone in the wilderness far from their homes, but nothing could persuade them to leave their prize until their baskets were filled. "Delicious meat! so good!" they exclaimed over and over again.

On every little eminence on their homeward journey they halted, formed a circle, and shouted. When within about a mile of the village, this telephone prevailed, and down the hill, pell-mell, came the village in force, men, women, and children with flaming torches, and yells of welcome. There was meat enough now to tide the people over the famine to the reaping time. This may seem a small matter, but it proved a strong tie in binding the people to their religious teacher.

XIV

OUR FIRST WHITE GUESTS

ERE a second year had passed in our new home, we received a note from our nearest white neighbor, Colonel Buckingham, saying that ten of the English gentlemen from the tea gardens lying along the base of the hills would like to come up and pay us a visit. Of course we returned a most cordial and hearty invitation. Although ten persons would be a large party for our limited accommodations, yet, as usual with travelers in India, they would bring their bedding. Nagas, always ready to lend a hand in our emergencies, were called in, and in no very long time bedsteads, seats, and other necessaries were provided, and the important question, " What shall we eat? " soon settled, when a young animal from our herd, dressed ready for use, hung in the " godown."

For only about four miles from Amguri was the path suitable for ponies, thence the guests must take to their feet. One ingenious planter, however, determining to further utilize his pony, passed around his own body a strap which he attached to the animal, and had only to keep his feet going while he was drawn along; but soon the path became too rough and rocky even for this mode of locomotion.

F

Our guests were expected for the accustomed midday India breakfast, but having frequently seen our Nagas go back and forth, they mistook the distance and the difficulties of travel, and it was past noon when two young men, the first of the party, arrived, their faces blood-red and dripping with perspiration; others followed in the same condition, quite exhausted, all declaring they had had no conception of either the distance or the roughness and steepness of the path. Another of the party came hurriedly, saying that a middle-aged gentleman, a barrister, recently out from England, was at the base of the hill utterly unable to make the last ascent. The villagers, indulging in a holiday in honor of this occasion, as well as to be in readiness for any desired service, were quite in their element for such an emergency, and soon settled the question of getting up our distinguished visitor. Several strong young men ran down the hill to the rescue, and placing a rattan rope around the body of the gentleman, proceeded to draw him up the hill.

We sat down to breakfast at three o'clock, a cheerful, social, hungry party. After breakfast our friends went out to view the charming scenery, of which they expressed great appreciation. They were also shown "about the town," examined the military barracks, the village stockade, gateways, and so on to the cemetery outside. Later followed afternoon tea and still later dinner. This was a delightful break in the monotony of our everyday life.

This visit occurred late in the dry season, before the setting in of the rains, while the mountain streams were dry and the springs low. With many baths—as to entertain guests in the tropics without baths would be like an Indian breakfast without curry—and the increased demand for water for general and culinary purposes, the villagers told us, when the party left, there was scarcely a vessel of water in the village.

Fifty rupees were left with us by Colonel Buckingham whereby came our first schoolhouse.

Later another gift from the same source " to be used as you see best for the good of the Nagas" helped to repair and furnish the chapel with benches. The iron standards were brought from Calcutta, while the Nagas hewed out the planks for seats.

The adjustment of the Nagas to these advanced accommodations was amusing. Some of the men looked for a moment, then stepped up on the seats and sat down on their feet. The women, a little more modest, stood, as if considering for a little what was most fitting to do; then some sat down properly, others put their children on the seats while they themselves sat on the floor in front. Soon, however, all accommodated themselves to the new arrangement with no little merriment and with much appreciation.

XV

RIPENING GRAIN

ON beginning our work among this people, two of the most intelligent men of the village were chosen to come to the bungalow morning by morning to talk with us, rather to permit us to pick from their mouths, or throats, it seemed, their unwritten language. We gave these men one rupee (thirty-three cents) each—very good pay—for eight lessons. They kept their account by creases on a rattan thrust in our bamboo wall; and whenever there were eight breaks they said, " Here, father, is not one rupee due us? "

In reducing the language to writing we used the Roman character. The expense of printing our first primer was borne by Mr. Godby's Bible class of boys of the First Baptist Church, Newark, N. J. On opening our first school the children came pouring in as if for a holiday; but, as soon as they understood that quiet and attention were the rule, all was changed. Then, to get them in at all, it was necessary to hold our session in the early morning, before the day's work in the field began and, even then, we were never certain whether they would be in the schoolroom or, like monkeys, in the trees, on the roofs of the houses or some other place. But gradually there came to be

84

some appreciation of what educated boys and girls might be and do.

A few larger girls whose work would not permit their attendance mornings, came each evening to the bungalow, chatting merrily, lighting their path with torches or firebrands. After an hour with books, sewing, and conversation about the new religion and other matters, the torches were brought to a blaze, a pleasant good-night salaam was given, and these bright, happy girls were off—girls whom any one might enjoy the effort to elevate!

One evening when the people were gathered in goodly numbers at the mission bungalow for the usual prayer meeting, Tungbangla, one of the schoolgirls, arose and said, " I believe on this Jesus, accept him as my only Saviour, and I wish to be numbered among his followers." Her's was the first Naga woman's voice ever heard making the great confession. How bright and beautiful, how hallowed seemed the dark and dingy room thus lightened by the presence of the life-giving Spirit!

Tungbangla and Noksangla, schoolgirl associates, were soon baptized, and these with another schoolgirl, were often heard in their own humble abodes at the hour for retiring offering up their simple petitions to the true God. Tungbangla became a valuable helper, teaching in our day-school, and visiting with me from house to house. Often our audiences were long rows of women, each hunting in the hair of the one before her. We frequently came upon some mother pressing a dying child to her bosom and screaming into its mouth, "O my baby, come back, come back." These wild people often shake the dying, set them upright, blow in their eyes to prevent their closing, and blow sparks up the nose to call back the departing spirit. When urged to allow their friends to lie quietly on their plank beds to pass away in peace, they think us unsympathetic and cold-hearted.

Tungbangla was the first in our parish to receive Christian marriage. We were called up early one morning for this wedding, in order that she and her chosen one might go out to the rice-field for the day's work. Her husband proving shiftless, lazy, and improvident, she applied to the village court for divorce. The court asked, "Did not the missionary marry you?" "Yes." "Then we can do nothing about it," was the verdict quickly rendered. Later they moved to Yazang village, where Tungbangla gathered a little day-school, and taught the Scriptures. On one of our visits several who had accepted the truth were baptized and organized into a little church, choosing as their pastor an elderly man from Molung, who served them for one dollar a month and his rice. Later this little flock built a chapel and a house for their preacher.

In returning from Yazang we found the river swollen, and there was much discussion as to how the Mem Sahib should be gotten over. "Too much cloth! Too much shoe and stocking!" they exclaimed. As the water reached only to their armpits, Mr. Clark said, "Oh, they'll take you over easily." Whereupon drawing myself up into as small a compass as possible, the strongest man of the party put his head under the bark band attached to my chair and lifted me well up on his shoulders. Another man was sent just in advance to pick the way and find a sure footing. Two more men, one on either side, kept close to my chair to serve in case of an emergency. It was a novel experience, and when shore was gained we felt like joining in the shouts that made the forest ring.

Tungbangla suffered a long, tedious illness, and became nearly blind, yet never lost sight of her Saviour. She ofttimes expressed great joy in anticipation of being with him, and frequently referred to the difference in her hope and that of a soul going out into the dark unknown. Years later, on one of our evangelistic tours to a distant village, a young miss, genteel in manner, with a quiet, pleasant face, clean and tidy, modestly inquired, "Mem Sahib, do you know me?" "Why, no, I have never been here before." Then came the reply, "Don't know me! Why, I am your Tungbangla's daughter." The two little girls left by this dear Christian were now grown to young womanhood. I advised that they be sent to our Impur school, and the eldest, Waeyila, has since been reported among the members of Impur church.

Our Molung village gradually grew to observe the Sabbath pretty generally as a day in which to abstain from the regular work of the week. When first approached on this subject, the reply was, " Why, father, do you mean for us not to reap on Sundays; to sit in our village one day in seven when the grain is ripe?"

Harvest time came; there had been a long " spell of catching weather," as the home farmers say; then followed a beautiful Sabbath morning, and we greatly feared the temptation to gather in the already over-ripe grain would be greater than these babes in the truth could resist. But to our surprise the attendance was larger than usual, and the following morning witnessed a fresh and early rush to the harvest fields. We many times observed this unusually early starting out on Monday mornings, and even the people themselves said they did more and better work and kept in better condition physically, for the rest of the one day in seven.

A printed letter in those early days reads:

" As I hear the voices in our prayer meetings of those who have been born anew, and watch their features soften, as they mirror the new hope, I no longer see the savages to whom we first came.

" An old-time leader in the evil ways of his people, valiant in war and taking much delight therein, is now one of our most substantial Christians, highly esteemed in his own village, and his words weighty in council.

" The Sunday services are well attended. The people are not allowed to smoke or spit inside the place of worship. As a Naga is scarcely a Naga without his pipe, he smokes until he reaches the door, then gives a good puff and puts his pipe—in his pocket? No, not at all, the pipe is placed in his belt, or laid near-by on the mat floor, and not infrequently a little child picks it up and takes a whiff. When one is late he may be accosted with, 'Did you stop in your house to fill your stomach?' When the preacher makes a particularly good point, there is frequently a response by a decided nod of the head, or in a half-audible tone, 'That's so,' 'Yes, that's a truth,' 'Yes, we ought to do thus and so.'

"Often when we come to the closing hymn, and God-hula pours out his rich, melodious voice in some inspiring song, the people catch fire (they all sing, the men making a very good bass); and warming up, draw nearer and nearer together, step by step, until all coming alongside, we truly realize, 'Blest be the tie that binds.'"

The room in our bungalow, becoming too small for our Sabbath congregations, we removed the chimney-less fire-hearth from the center of the room to one corner, thus much enlarging the seating capacity.

After the harvest our proposition to build a house for the Lord was well received. The whole village was set to work, the building went rapidly up, and our modest little bamboo structure was dedicated free of debt, a contribution by the Nagas to the American Baptist Missionary Union. The first seats were of usual Naga style, blocks of wood, or a long slab for "a family pew." When guests from neighboring villages chanced to drop in, the ever-present extra seat was supplied by their drawing the axe from its sheath, a Nâga's seat in any emergency by day, and his pillow by night. In the new chapel our congregations increased very perceptibly. Some people came into this more public place of worship who had hesitated to enter into the closer quarters. Many loungers too sat just outside the door, where they might enjoy their pipe and catch bits of the truth.

It was suggested that, after the reaping, we should see what a harvest home festival would bring. Due notice was given and a certain Sabbath fixed upon, that all who were inclined might bring their gifts. Mats, one for the white rice, and one for the red, were spread in the open space in front of the pulpit, and two generous piles of "paddy" were the result. This festival has been established in some of our churches as an annual offering. The practice also of regular Sunday contributions of small measures of rice is now common, and baskets are set near the pulpit to receive it. A very pretty sight it is to see the people, especially the women, as they enter the chapel door, deposit their little gifts. An egg is frequently found in the contribution box. It was customary with the heathen Ao Nagas to accompany every act of worship with a gift. Consequently not very much instruction was required to induce the people to contribute of their means for religious purposes, and to lay aside at daily meals a small gift for the Lord's work.

Ere twelve months had passed we repaired one bright Sabbath morning to nature's own baptistery beneath the shade of overhanging vines and branches —a wild, pretty spot, a most suitable Jordan, from which seven of these hitherto bold warriors were raised to newness of life. Later, as we gathered to " do this in remembrance of Me " there was christened the pretty communion service given by the Sunday-schools of the two home churches of the first missionaries to this people.

The young colony grew and prospered. Families from other villages gradually came in and we soon numbered a hundred houses; yet with these came also demon worship and heathen rites. A noted sorceress came and supported herself by her divinations. Christianity, however, kept the ascendency. Gradually other villages, seeing our prosperity, began asking for teachers, and the Nagas not being sufficiently advanced, a few Assamese Christians were called for evangelistic and educational work. Zilli, one of Doctor Bronson's former helpers in Assam, with his wife Jointa, joined us in the work at Molung, and both proved valuable assistants.

Later, on a Sunday evening, we were very unexpectedly invited to a Sunday-school concert, managed entirely by preacher Zilli. The bamboo chapel was well lighted with lamps and lanterns; the congregation assembled, and the day-school and Sunday-school children came marching in singing in broken English—but it sounded sweetly—"We're marching to Zion, beautiful Zion." There were recitations in English and Naga, interspersed with singing in both languages. Several young men took part, acquitting themselves with credit. The singing of "Bringing in the sheaves" was a suggestive climax to this day of beginnings.

XVI

PROGRESS AND PERIL

A S time went on different villages began inviting us, some even volunteering to come and bring us. Our cold season tourings were thus much increased. With our evangelistic helpers, servants, and carriers, bearing chairs, bedding, pots and pans, dishes, lanterns, kerosene oil, and food in numerous bundles, all marching in single file over the steeps and through the gullies, we presented a long and picturesque procession. Frequently village chiefs on important business would accompany us, dressed in their finest cloths and war finery, thus adding, with their necessary attendants, considerable dignity to our party.

Arriving at our destination, a cup of tea would soon refresh us, and in a short time we were set up in housekeeping and ready for the reception which always awaited us; then followed preaching, visiting the women in their homes, ministering to the sick, and striving in every way to reach the people.

The eagerness of the villages to receive us was such that soon we had only to send a messenger a day or two in advance in order to find a new, fresh, little bamboo house, furnished with bedstead and table, awaiting us, with a pleasant little porch over our front door and a cookhouse just outside. Did we chance to reach a village too late for a new house to be made ready by evening, the public hall with fresh mats for walls and flooring was at our service, or the dwelling of one of the first families would be vacated for us.

Good congregations were always obtainable in almost no time in the cold season, the people living mostly in the street, doing their work in the sunshine. To many, the old, old story sounded strange and sweet when heard for the first time. A pause by the preacher was taken as an opportunity for all sorts of questions, either pertaining to or widely diverse from the subject. As I went among the women, one would ask:

" Is your mother living? "

" Yes."

" She must be awfully old."

" Have you any children? "

Then as the story was related of the one angel child above, there would come from a sympathetic, sorrowing mother:

" Beautiful, beautiful words, how sweet to hear! I wish I knew how to believe them. Did you come all the way to tell us this? "

As we continued to speak of the home above and of salvation through Jesus alone, another would say:

" Do hear her sweet words! "

Another calls out, " How is your cloth woven? "

" Do they wear such cloth in heaven? "

" How smooth your hair is; do you have lice in it? "

Answering this last, several voices exclaimed: " Do tell ! What medicine do you use? "

On leaving a certain village, just after passing through the gateway of the stockade, we came to a strange little bamboo hut with bones of various animals and broken cooking pots strewed around.

" What is this? " we inquired.

" Oh ! that is Leezaba's (the evil deity's) cookhouse."

The sacrifices made for him in the village for sickness and misfortune did not seem to avail, and this house had been built solely for him. Portions of animals slain for feasts were placed here for Leezaba, that he might cook for himself, and thus perhaps be satisfied.

At Wamaken village, we were very proud as we listened to our Christian Edeeba's address. He began away back with the story of the creation, and step by step came down to the great sacrifice for sin; indeed quite an oration. The people listened. " Tell us more," they said. " Our minds are all dark; we have no torch to guide us." One woman exclaimed, " Oh, yes, that is just what Assamese Godhula has been telling us, and we want to throw away this Leezaba worship and serve the true God."

Unger, a strongly fortified, plucky little village, right on a rough, rocky summit, was entered by crossing on a single tree trunk over a broad ditch stuck thickly with sharp bamboo spikes.

The farther we traveled the larger the villages and

more fertile the land. Yet the people, leaving the beautiful plateaus on mountain crests, chose for their homes the rocky, rugged peaks as more easily defended.

On one of our tours I was taken quite ill and, unable to be carried in a chair; the Nagas, ever fertile in ways and means, improvised a dhuli in which I could lie down and be borne by four. The Nagas, however, being unaccustomed to this sort of partnership, it proved a genuine " Humpty-dumpty " experience; the conveyance frequently catching on a stump or scraping against a projecting rock. The weather grew threatening, and we were two days' march from Molung, but, by pressing on with relays of men, we arrived at the end of our journey about midnight. A severe attack of the grippe was upon us both and no physician near.

Again, Mr. Clark and Godhula on tour chanced to stop in a large village through which an English survey party had previously passed. Soon after smallpox in a severe form broke out; the party was charged with bringing the scourge, and in consequence the village bound itself with an oath that a European head should pay the penalty. Unfortunately for Mr. Clark, these oath-bound warriors knew no difference between an English official and the humble messenger of the cross. Mr. Clark and Godhula soon became cognizant of the situation; it was indeed hazardous; what was to be done? While praying for guidance and protection, the answer came in the very unexpected arrival of a large body of strong, stalwart young men friendly to our Molung village. The safety of the mission party assured, a quiet, peaceful night was passed and the gospel preached to the people.

On another occasion Mr. Clark, while touring, noticed that his Naga attendant was considerably excited and careful to keep well in front of him on the path. Stopping for the night, the attendance at their meeting in the village was small and the inattention and restlessness of the people created suspicions which were well-grounded. When the meeting broke up and the missionary was about to retire several men came in and, after talking in low tones with one another and addressing a few unintelligible questions to my husband, went out; others came conducting themselves in a similar manner. Some plot evidently was under consideration. Finally, as if the project had been abandoned, all was quiet. The following morning it was learned that the kidnapping of Mr. Clark and his helper had been seriously contemplated.

But there was other than strictly religious progress in our parish. With our sparse house furnishings, anything in the way of additions and conveniences was very much appreciated. There were no closets, bureaus, or shelves even. Everything was in trunks and boxes standing on the floor, and it was bend and stoop and kneel whenever anything was wanted, while a great pile of packing cases, in which came our Calcutta stores, was fast accumulating at the back of the house.

G

It was suggested that these boxes be brought in, piled and matched as well as possible. The suggestion was accepted, but, as usual, very much improved upon by Mr. Clark. He said the Nagas could knock the boxes to pieces, and he, at odd times, could match the boards and make one huge closet, if it would be acceptable without planing. Oh, certainly, by all means. Hence in due time there arose in our bedroom a wardrobe with shelves, and never in all my life was I so proud of a piece of furniture. It was so interesting too, as I awoke in the morning and my eyes resting on this cabinet, I read, " From Planter's Stores, Dibrugarh "; " Sykes & Co., Calcutta "; " Care J. Buckingham, Amguri Tea Estate "; " Great Eastern General Stores "; " Standard Oil, U. S. A." Ah, on these last letters my eyes were wont to linger while I delighted in pleasant reminiscences.

Then the old bedstead built with the house seemed to be growing harder, and we called in the Nagas and had a new one made, of thinner, more flexible, springy bamboo splints.

XVII

TROUBLE ON OUR PATH

I HAD been spending a little time at Sibsagor when my husband came to accompany me back to the hills. The elephant was at the door, we had said our good-byes, when two Nagas hurriedly and excitedly appeared, bringing the intelligence that two men had been speared on the path between our village and Dekha Haimong, causing serious alarm to our people. Other messengers also soon followed bringing a note from Colonel Buckingham, advising Mr. Clark's immediate return, leaving me at Sibsagor, as there was grave trouble and much excitement among the Nagas.

Mr. Clark hastened at once to the hills. He found matters even worse than had been represented. Besides the spearing of the two men reported, two Molung men had been killed and there was much ambushing by the enemy along our route, evidently designed to cut off our communication with Assam, which in this hostile country would never do. This path belonged especially to Molung village, and according to Naga usage, other villagers had no right to travel thereon without permission. This precaution was necessary, as this was our only direct communication with the plain.

After learning the facts and finding out the guilty

party, Mr. Clark, with two of our faithful and most
influential men of the village, returned to Sibsagor.
The matter was brought to the attention of the chief
commissioner of Assam, asking the protection of the
British government to Europeans on its frontier, and
to interfere on our behalf in this recent serious trouble.
The chief commissioner very kindly authorized Deputy Commissioner Colonel Campbell, who had charge
of the Sibsagor district extending to the base of the
hills, to investigate and settle this affair.

Messengers were despatched by Colonel Campbell
to Temlu, the offending village, demanding its head
men to appear before her majesty's court at Sibsagor.
They came, confessed to the act, and were fined one
hundred and fifty rupees, about fifty dollars, to be paid
in seventeen days, two of the head men being detained
in Sibsagor jail as hostages until the whole amount
should be brought in. The Temlu men declared that
the village could not meet such a demand. In this
threatening phase of matters I was not allowed to return to the hills, and Mr. Clark went back at his own
risk.

Twelve days later Temlu Nagas appeared in Sibsagor with forty rupees, asserting with great positive-
ness that no more money could be raised though they
be punished to the utter destruction of their village.
This is a common ruse among Orientals. But Colonel
Campbell was unrelenting in his decision, and the Temlu men, finding it was useless to hold out longer, came

within the prescribed time, bringing the full measure of their penalty. Colonel Campbell required two of the head men to sign an agreement by their own mark, to the effect that no further depredations should be committed on the Molung paths, and that the missionaries should not be molested.

With a light heart I was soon off to meet my husband at Amguri, and proceeded with him to our home among these warriors. In honor of my return, also to show appreciation of Mr. Clark's services in the recent unpleasant affair, the chief men of Molung dressed in their finest were down with Mr. Clark to meet me. As I remarked, " With such trouble on our path, how can I go up?" they replied, " Why, Mem Sahib, the whole ' kingdom ' is down to take care of you." And sure enough here was the entire village force ready to do us free service.

We started off with our long procession, body-guard in front of us, body-guard in rear of us, body-guard alongside of us. It was the beginning of the rainy season and leeches were plentiful; although in a chair on a man's back far above the reach of these troublesome pests, yet one man was detailed especially to protect me. It was amusing to see the people with a jerk and a fling throw off these blood suckers. One man carried tobacco juice in a small bamboo—this is quite customary when traveling in the rains—and occasionally passed through the procession swabbing down their bare legs and feet, thus causing the leeches to curl up

and drop. Frequently Europeans traveling in these regions are quite disabled by the bites of these little creatures. Safe on the mountain crest again, a most hearty
welcome from all awaited us, and we hoped to resume
our work unmolested.

XVIII

IN November, 1880, we were glad to welcome to our rude home Rev. C. D. King, of the Assam mission. We will let him speak for himself.

"Oh, you ought to have seen it all ! Your hearts too would have thrilled. You should first have lived for a few months among the Nagas in some portion of their own great stretch of wild, grand, forest-begirt hills, to appreciate what I have seen during a two weeks' visit here in Mr. Clark's vast parish. There is much that suggests a comparison with our own North American Indians, as they were in the days of their prowess. Human skulls here are as honorable trophies as ever were scalps to the American savage. Villages that can display but few skulls are held in contempt. Among such people as this, it is a matter of no small encouragement to see even one Christian church and one nominally Christian village, keeping the Sabbath and holding itself aloof from all the petty wars that rage about it; a village which, without skulls or other warlike distinctions, compels the respect of others because it is Christian. Such is this village of Molung. It is literally a city set on a hill, and we are having just now ample proof that it cannot be hid.

"I wish I could describe the first religious meeting I attended here, and those of the Sabbath Day which followed. Can you realize how hearing representatives of all the thousands on these wild hills humbly praying to Yehovah Yeesu Kreesta, and feeling sure of the sympathy of his brethren, would quicken the ardor of your own soul? And now listen to their singing. These deep, guttural, bass voices, and these strange-sounding words never before written, till brought together in these hymns, what a new charm they give to the familiar tunes, 'Lead me, O thou great Jehovah,' 'How Firm a Foundation,' 'My Faith Looks up to Thee.'

"Sunday evening, and the one little Sunday-school of all Naga land convenes—Mrs. Clark and her school-girls. They come, tripping along with a free, wide-awake air; many of them with black, home-made tobacco pipes in their mouths, which they remove at once on entering the chapel. The numerous small brass bells strung around the necks of the fidgety little ones keep up a constant jingle.

"Here are girls just blooming into young womanhood; girls that in the valley would ere their age have been married. There is one whose face you will never forget, Tungbangla, to whom reference has already been made. Her voice was the first among Naga women to say, 'Let me be with you on the Lord's side.' She and one other, a young married woman, also a member of Mrs. Clark's school, were baptized last August. Oh, how quickly all the sacrifices of these past years faded into nothingness! And how glorious seemed the reward when these two young women were known to be heirs of the life everlasting.

"This evening a woman, who has of late been a very attentive listener at the meetings, makes her first confession of having 'thrown away every vestige of the old religion,' and tells how she prays every night to the true God, and finds great joy in trusting in Yeesu Kreesta. Her husband responds audibly, 'Amen,' and tells her she is doing right.

"Would I could make you see Tungbangla's face, as, seated on a low block, quite near her new-found fellow-pilgrim, she watches and listens with dilated eyes and parted lips, and many a little gesture of deep satisfaction and intense interest. I would also have you note the commanding and interesting face of Imrong, who can hardly be restrained from putting words into the woman's mouth, to tell her how she feels, while manifesting his own satisfaction in audible exclamations. All followed with interest the brief Sunday-school lesson, and Imrong, being asked about the state of things at Merangkong, his pent-up enthusiasm burst forth. 'At Merangkong on Sundays, hundreds of the people, men, women, and children, come together to hear what I can tell them about the Christian religion.' Godhula, rejoicing, takes it up, 'Mem Sahib, Christianity will eat them up.' And the Mem Sahib herself is by no means insensible to the thrilling influences of the occasion. How often she has said, 'Oh,

if these people would only manifest a little more enthusiasm!' But it is their nature to be slow and phleg-
matic. Imrong's fire seems a miracle. How wonderfully the prayer for laborers has been answered! Our
hearts burned within us as later we talked and prayed
over these mighty transformations, and particularly of
one man who, when asked why he wished to be baptized, answered, 'I want to be washed from all my old
religion, father, and have your God for my God, and
obey him in all things.'"

At heart Imrong may not have been more devoted
to the cause of Christ, or in his life more faithful or
true than some of the other Christian Nagas; but he
had the fervor, the zeal, the enthusiasm many seemed
to lack and which we so longed to see in this people.
I thought him about the homeliest man in all the village, very tall, muscular, square-shouldered, angular,
loose-jointed, and such hands and feet! His deep,
heavy, sonorous voice made the forests ring; and whenever he was deputed to herald a public notice through
the village, no one having ears could fail to hear.
Whenever in our journeyings he was my bearer I felt
I had a tower of strength beneath me. I could truly
say, "I loved him like a brother." Imrong finally removed to Merangkong, but never resumed the old
demon worship or took any part in the village feasts
or sacrifices. Mr. Clark once asked him, "Imrong, do
you make offerings to Leezaba nowadays when your
wife or children are ill?" With those two great

hands uplifted, and with an expression of horror, he exclaimed, " Never, father, never, no never! "

Sitting by my window one day I heard the peculiar sound of axes rattling in their sheaths on the Nagas' backs, and the patter, patter of many bare feet. Sure enough visitors were coming, and such a procession! I had counted into the nineties when our brother Imrong stepped up to the door with his usual ardor and enthusiasm, while back of him stood two hundred and fifty men from Merangkong who had stopped, at his suggestion, to express anew their regard and affection for " father " and the " Mem Sahib."

Going down the hillside one morning we were surprised to see that a huge boulder, long thought to be the abode of demons, was broken. Formerly no one would go near it; but the boys taught in our day and Sunday schools gradually began to climb over it and sharpen their hatchets on it, and now, doubtless, some of these young dissenters had struck the fatal blow—a blow too, full of meaning.

Oh, how we rejoiced when Sentimong, after relapsing to heathen rites through the persuasions of his pagan wife, broke completely down in our prayer meeting one evening, pleading, " I am so sorry; the Saviour's face has been turned away from me; the Christian teacher has had no smiles for me; all has been dark; O Jesus, forgive me."

With like joy we thanked God for another victory when Mangkorepba and his wife made not the costly offerings we feared they would in time of sickness, and, grateful for their recovery, gave glory to God in altered lives, and asked that they might witness to the same, with others, in baptism.

My journal of those old-time days reads:

"You can hardly realize how civilized, comparatively, our Nagas are becoming. Around-the-world tourists chancing to give us a call would wonder what our parishioners once were. They do not exactly come in and ask for the latest telegrams from England and America when our mail-bag arrives; but they are anxious to know all we may choose to tell them of its contents. You should hear their exclamations of wonder as they turn the pages of " Harper's Weekly "! They are in a new world of which they never dreamed. When our new missionary map from Boston was hung up before them, " Wah! wah! wah! father, what does it speak? " uttered in reverent exclamations gave opportunity for such a lesson as led old Deacon Scubungallumba to drop his head and mutter almost under his breath, " Ish, Ish! how great we have thought ourselves, as though we were the big part of all creation."

Later literary and school work going on apace, Mr. Clark requested that a hand printing-press be sent out from Boston. A much larger one than was expected came very near proving a black elephant on our hands. The Nagas, now eager for every new evidence of their progress civilization-ward, voluntarily contributed two whole days to the tremendous task of bringing it to our hilltop. In 1885 the Gospels of Matthew and John were ready to put into the hands of those who could read. A new and enlarged collection of hymns, the history of Joseph, and more school books were added. We never can tell our joy when the young men and women in our congregation began intelligently to handle the Scriptures and hymn books! What did it matter if sometimes the books were held upside down by the older ones who did not wish to be outdone; their honest pride spoke volumes. Of what account were any sacrifices for this people now glad to have us with them and eager for the printed page!

XIX

THE Molung people, jealous of our growing interest in the large and prosperous village of Merangkong, argued, "Those people have as many wars as there are hairs on a Naga's head. The path thither is extremely difficult and unsafe. Why talk of going over there?"

However, we decided to make the venture and a large number of our Molung folks offered to go with us. Again and again we were obliged to tunnel our way through long reaches of vines, intertwining creepers and overarching branches—a veritable subway. Approaching the village, such a climb! Passing the sentinels on the watch-tower at the gateway, a characteristic welcome helped to dispel the weariness of the journey. Chickens began to squawk; rice, chillies, yams, and sugar-cane galore were spread before us; and in the house placed at our disposal we were quickly "at home," but we asked to be excused from the four men proffered to occupy the room with us at night for protection, preferring the risk to Naga snoring.

Some time previous to this visit there had been found at the gateway of Dekha Haimong, the mother village

NAGA VILLAGE IN THE DISTANCE

of Molung, a broken pongee (a sharpened, dangerous, usually poisoned bamboo splint) and a quenched torch, —an unmistakable declaration of war, placed there by the Temlu people. This apparently failing to arouse the Ao people, a little later there was perpetrated the dastardly ambush attack on the Molung path referred to in a previous chapter, thus showing clearly the purpose of Temlu to open war on Molung. Ostensibly repenting this act, Temlu head men had for some time been sending for Mr. Clark to visit them. The request becoming more and more urgent, Mr. Clark, after conferring with Molung and Merangkong people, decided to go, and accompanied by Godhula, with fifteen or twenty Merangkong men as body-guard, proceeded on this uncertain mission.

The path was a dangerous war route. Some of the party armed with spears and shields marched before Mr. Clark, while others followed close after. Scarcely four miles were covered before a halt was called. "Father, there is ambushing all along this path; if we keep our heads on we shall do well. What do you say? Is it forward or back?" A moment later one exclaims, "We can't stop long to talk here; it must be one way or the other at once!" Forward, was the word, but cautiously in solid phalanx. Passing a sharp turn in the path, spears came suddenly flying pell-mell between the men and even between the legs of one man. At Mr. Clark's order the one gun in the party was fired into the jungle with the effect of quickly dispersing the supposed enemy. Baskets, cloths, and other articles strewed the path, their owners nowhere to be seen. Then followed shouts and calls, and lo, from their hiding-place in the jungle the Temlu men stood before them! Surprised and frightened by the sudden appearance of this formidable procession, they had thrown their spears in self-defense. Soon all was satisfactorily explained and the parties marched on together.

At the base of Temlu Hill it was suggested that a delegation be sent in advance to inform the village and bring word whether or not they would be received. In answer the head village official, with his attendants, came running down as fast as the dignity of his office would permit, his face wreathed in smiles; indeed this was all he might be said to wear. Every tree-top and shrub was filled with men and boys as Mr. Clark and his attendants were escorted with great deference and honor past sentinels at the gateway and up through the village street, and there was nothing lacking in the lavish entertainment of the entire party.

The past rehearsed, the Temlu men confessed to ambuscading the Molung path, but insisted that the deed was instigated by a treacherous neighboring village for which they were only the "catspaw." Much regret was expressed for the act, and a desire shown to be friends with the "Sahib" and the "Molungnungers."

Already the shadows were lengthening, when suddenly there appeared in their midst enemies of the

Merangkong people. "What was to be done now?" Although these new-comers were few in number, they might hasten back to their own near-by village and rally for an attack on Mr. Clark's party while returning to Merangkong. Special effort was made, therefore, to retain these men while the Merangkong party should quickly disappear in the darkness. It was not safe to carry torches, so the travelers proceeded, feeling their way as best they could. It was a terrible experience; but a happy, praiseful company marched into Merangkong village after midnight.

During Mr. Clark's absence fifteen armed men guarded the little bamboo quarters of the missionary's wife, and escorted her in walks through the village. Two of our schoolgirls were with me, and we visited many of these dark, dark homes.

We were now in the heart of the Ao tribe, among the big war villages, three days removed from any white face; large parties of travelers numbering several hundred were constantly coming and going, and in addition to preaching the gospel there was much diplomatic work. Supposed abodes of the spirits were numerous and skulls everywhere, a dozen or more adorning many a doorway.

In one of our walks through the village we came to a large, comfortable looking house with the entire front wall removed, and across this space, hung on bamboo poles, were men's and women's clothes, jewelry, skeins of yarn, unfinished cloth from the loom,

H

cooking utensils, implements of husbandry, everything worn and used by a well-to-do family. We were told that a young man of the household had been carried off by a tiger, hence the old story of sin and an abandoned home, as told in a former chapter. Although desirous of obtaining these fine ornaments for curios, we hesitated, as to do so would cause us to become sinful in the eyes of the people. We consulted the officials. "Why, yes," they said, "take them if you dare," but we did not remove them until the time for our departure. When we were ready to return to Molung no one came to take our loads. We called and waited, grew impatient, sent again and again for our bearers. Finally we were told that with the accursed articles in the luggage no one would carry it. On Mr. Clark's showing them the jewelry in our little handbag one of our Christians immediately took it, the best possible proof of his sincerity in abandoning old-time customs.

A large escort from Merangkong accompanied us to the river. Going down the deep descent from the village gate the chief kept close to my bearer, pointing out the steps, and in the most difficult places stood with outstretched arms in case of an accident. What a relief that no such casualty occurred!

Later, several were baptized at Merangkong and a little church organized. The few gathered in from this hard field speaks volumes to one who has lived to see it. A young Naga evangelist and his wife from the

Impur Training School are now there as religious and day-school teachers, and others are being gathered in.

On his return from a furlough in America, Mr. Clark writes: "The last annual meeting of the Ao Naga Association—1904—was held at Merangkong. As the place was not so central and measles were prevailing in many villages, the attendance was not so large as usual (there are generally from two hundred to three hundred persons present). The church is weak, yet hospitality was unstinted. The Association touched high-water mark as to spiritual power and devotion. The main sermon was preached by your former schoolboy, Samar, and showed considerable thought, was elevated in tone and delivered with much oratorical power."

XX

OPPORTUNITIES BLOOD-BOUGHT

FROM Ao land, crossing the Lhota tribe, a distance of one hundred miles or more, are the powerful, roaming Angamis. In the days of the old Assam kings these Angamis were much given to looting Assamese villages, carrying off cattle, goats, and dogs, and not infrequently a much prized human head. For this reason the English government was compelled to station a resident political agent on one of the lower Angami hills in the village of Samaguting, near the main route to the plain. English officers with native troops also went farther into the hills and established headquarters at Kohima, one of the largest villages and centrally located. This military encroachment aroused the war villages in the interior, and an attack on the English was begun at Samaguting. Kohima was also besieged by thousands of hostile Nagas and was only relieved by an increased English force.

There was a general uprising throughout the entire Angami tribe with the purpose of killing or driving out every one connected with British rule. One English officer and several sepoys were killed. Without pen, ink, paper, telegraph or telephone, the news of these events spread like wildfire from mountain peak to

ANGAMI WARRIORS

mountain peak, from tribe to tribe. The air was full of rumors and the people were at high tension. The alarm reaching the plains, Colonel Campbell, English magistrate of Sibsagor District, and Colonel Buckingham, of Amguri, each sent special messengers urging us to flee at once. But we were accustomed to war rumors and decided to stand by our own people and quietly await events.

The issue of this war was the entire subjugation of the Angami tribe, the annexation of their country, and permanent occupation of Kohima by a strong military force. This occurred in March, 1880, and about this time the Lhota tribe, lying between the Angamis and the Aos, was taken in, thus bringing English rule to our Ao border.

Mr. Clark, long anticipating this splendid opening, had importuned the Missionary Union to send a man to the Angami Nagas, with Kohima, at an elevation of four thousand five hundred feet, as missionary headquarters.

Rev. C. D. King was appointed, but not being permitted to proceed at once to Kohima, stopped at the lower village, Samaguting. Here Mrs. King soon joined him, and just in time to experience the terrors of an attack which compelled them to take refuge within the English stockade; and even from this shelter they were soon compelled to flee for their lives; but immediately the conflict was ended and the British flag unfurled over Kohima they hastened there.

Up to 1885 fifty-one Nagas and three Assamese had been baptized in our Ao Naga field. The Gospels of Matthew and John, the story of Joseph, a catechism, a collection of gospel hymns, and elementary school books had been published in the Ao tongue, and schools with Assamese teachers, who also served as evangelists, had been opened in several villages.

In January of that year Rev. and Mrs. S. W. Rivenburg arrived at Molung, and in May following Mr. Clark took his first home furlough after sixteen years in Assam. Six weeks later Mr. Rivenburg wrote of their not expecting to see a white face for the next six months, and of receiving mail only once in two weeks, but they were happy, and during their stay at Molung twenty-four persons were baptized and the kingdom advanced in many ways.

On our return to Assam in 1886, the missionaries were assembled for a jubilee conference in celebration of a half-century of mission work in Assam. In view of the early departure of the Kings for America, it was decided that the Rivenburgs should succeed them at Kohima, thus leaving us alone again among the Aos.

We found the work in a prosperous condition, with many pleasant surprises awaiting us. Mr. Rivenburg had availed himself of the doors and windows of an old abandoned mission bungalow in the plains, and utilized them in place of the sagging, scraping mats that had so annoyed us. Safely back in this comfortable home, renewed in strength and encouraged by the

HOME OF DOCTOR AND MRS. RIVENBURG—KOHIMA

sympathy and appreciation of the home churches, we joyfully resumed our life of isolation.

Dr. and Mrs. Rivenburg have remained at Kohima, toiling faithfully amid many difficulties, reducing the language to writing and doing much evangelistic, literary, and medical work. For the last Doctor Rivenburg qualified himself by a medical course during their first furlough in America.

The work of the Rivenburgs has appealed to the government, which has given them an excellent building site; a twenty years' lease of another piece of land on which stand two buildings, admirably adapted for school purposes; a monthly grant-in-aid of fifty-five rupees to help maintain the school; and generous grants for printing of Scripture translations, school books, and medical works prepared by Doctor Rivenburg. The missionaries at Kohima are now housed in a new and comfortable bungalow, and are rejoicing in fresh additions to their little band of Christians and the prosperity of their growing school, now numbering upwards of a hundred pupils.

XXI

FROM THE BATTLE-AXE TO THE BRITISH FLAG

IN 1885 the English government assumed suzerainty over the Ao Naga tribe. A strong military force marched the length and breadth of Ao territory, demanding of all the villages cessation from war. This edict was scarcely credited by the people. "This is only a big raid to get filled up," they said; and, still set on honors won by spilling human blood, continued their petty warfares, ambuscades, and plundering raids, involving costly English expeditions, with constant excitement, agitation, and unrest throughout the land.

Not readily comprehending their true relations to this new order, nor knowing just how much authority was left them for settling village crimes and inter-village broils, they asked: "Who is this Rani (queen) that she should reign over us?" "Are not some of us of royal blood?" "Have not we kings?" Again and again there came ambassadors from different villages to counsel with Mr. Clark; some, cognizant of their own misdeeds, would plead for his intercession on their behalf, and all begged for a written testimony of their peaceable conduct and good-will. It was amusing to see what confidence they suddenly had in a written statement, though none of them could read.

120

Just at dusk one evening there appeared before our door twenty warriors from Kansang village, which a few months previous had plotted to cut up an English officer and a small force of ten sepoys stopping there for the night. Rumors having reached us of this conspiracy, our Assamese helper, Zilli, was speedily despatched to apprise the party that there was danger. The officer, not pleased with his reception by this village, and finding that it was by one certain path and no other that the village proposed to escort him on his journey, decided that was not the route for him, and hastened on his way to safer British territory. This proved a wise act. Kansang, not having the courage to commit the dastardly deed, had enlisted men from villages across the Ao border to ambush this path. In anticipation of being called upon to answer for this, these Kansang ambassadors had come for the intercession of the missionary.

About midnight there came a heavy rap-tap at our door. Waramong men in great distress were there; their village had been fined for delinquency in furnishing load-carriers to a government expedition, and as they had just helped a neighboring village out of similar trouble, they were without money wherewith to meet the like demand upon themselves. Although Mr. Clark was absent, the needful rupees were given, in full confidence of repayment.

One village visited by this military expedition had been fined one hundred dollars for decoying into it four men and beheading them, and the surrender of the murderers required. Four poor, sickly, miserable men were brought before the English magistrate, confessed the crime, and were received as the supposed culprits, yet not without suspicion. Under pretense of moving camp, orders were given to assemble the entire village. When all were gathered in the presence of the military, the village was surrounded by a squad of sepoys, and under penalty of the complete destruction of the village and all their possessions three of the real murderers were produced. These were found to belong to the most prominent families of the village, hence the ruse of substitutes, which had been bought. The fourth of the guilty party having escaped, his house was destroyed and its rebuilding forbidden. The three guilty men were tried before the Sibsagor civil magistrate and sentenced for life to the Andaman Islands, an English convict settlement. Some villages, from fear of the new rule, came bringing in their slaves, proposing to place them in the missionary's care. From our hilltop during these military expeditions we often watched the flames of villages leaping upwards like tongues of fire.

The officers in command of these armed touring parties were ever glad to avail themselves of Mr. Clark's experience from long residence here, and time and again was he requested to meet the military at different points and travel with them. Striking was the contrast of the missionary, formerly attended only by his little staff of volunteers to the King of kings, now setting out with Her Majesty's armed corps. We gladly embraced such opportunities, and often sent supplies from our larder and vegetables and flowers from our garden to cheer the English officials marching through lands so barren. One day a telegram came—the wires, two men—the despatch respectfully, perhaps superstitiously, inserted in the slit end of a stick about three feet long. It proved to be an official order for load-carriers from Molung to meet an expedition and bring them on their way hither, where they would temporarily halt with us. The " fatted calf " was soon awaiting the hungry guests, whose coming meant so much in preparing the highway for the gospel.

In June, 1888, only three years after peace had been proclaimed in Ao land, a big tribe across the border, finding its tillable lands insufficient for its needs, began attacks on our frontier villages. In these attacks the large village, Mungsemdi, suffered most, losing by one invasion over one hundred and fifty men. Another village, Lungdang, lost fifty, and but for the presence of the English government, doubtless the conquest of the upper portion of the Ao tribe would have been achieved.

The news of this terrible raid upon two of the largest villages on the border of our tribe spread like wildfire from village to village throughout the entire land, and there was even greater excitement and commotion than we had experienced when foreign control was first announced. Some of our Molung village officials, returning from a ten days' tour through that part of the tribe, confirmed the report and told us of the great suffering through homes destroyed and granaries burned.

The border village, Suzu, was attacked, six men killed, and one carried away alive; the last considered a great achievement. Later, ambassadors from another frontier village came to us in great distress, having received a message from these same marauders to the effect that in six days they would pay them a visit. We could but pity these poor people, although we knew that it was but a short time since they too were on the war-path, glorying in the acquisition of fresh heads. They desired to be represented as friendly to the missionary and favorable to the English government.

English headquarters in Assam was notified of this disturbance, and one hundred and twenty sepoys from Sibsagor arrived in our village, and tarried with us for a night en route as a guard for the menaced border. This created quite an excitement, seemingly bringing the war to our very door. The sepoys were camped just below our bungalow, and their chit-chat in Assamese was really music to our ears, and cheered and enlivened our hearts, notwithstanding their serious errand.

In December, 1888, Lieutenant Maxwell, from Dibrugarh, Assam, with seventy frontier police, arrived at Molung, en route to the very heart of the enemy's country. We welcomed them heartily and sent them on their way with additional comforts.

From beyond the border, Mr. Davis, Deputy Commissioner of the Naga Hills, wrote: " We arrived here all right on the 6th. No opposition. The Noksens had big stones all ready to roll down upon our heads, but they had not the pluck to stop and cut the rattan ropes by which they were held. The villagers fired their own houses as we approached."

After the expedition had returned from the scene of the raid, Captain McIntyre wrote us as follows: " You must take for granted that everywhere the paths were stuck with bamboo spikes, and bow-and-arrow traps set. As we were nearing Noksen village, a trap went off, the arrow passing between Mr. Porteous and myself without hitting either of us.

" At Yeno, the Nagas strove to drive us back by threats and shouts, but retired as we approached. They set fire to their village; but as there was no wind, only their granaries burned.

" Santok appeared near, and we went on, never expecting any particular resistance, but found Nagas intrenched behind a long, thick wall, and a shower of arrows was let fly at us, yet no one was hit. We began with a volley, and were greatly surprised to find the Nagas would not halt. Some one must be killed, and my men were handicapped by the high wall in front. A Naga showed himself, firing a cross-bow from the corner of the intrenchment, and taking a rifle, I bowled him over, and my men fixing bayonets, we went up the hill with a hurrah. The Nagas bolted, setting fire to their village and completely destroying it.

" Great preparations had been made for entering Mozung-Jamee, the stronghold of old warriors of this raiding tribe. They lay in ambush on the path. Mr. Maxwell, taking our advance, charged them, and the Mozungas bolted without much show of resistance, leaving three or four dead on the field. Mozung-Jamee is about one mile long, with five political wards, all stuck with sharp bamboo spikes round and round with great care, and with very precarious bridges over deep ditches, also filled with spikes. One sepoy lost his head and hands at the water ghat, and another was speared through the leg by these Mozunga men. Poisoned arrow-traps were found set everywhere."

This punitive expedition visited eleven villages, nine of which were left in complete ruins, while two were partly destroyed. The most of the villages were burned by the people themselves. In the following April, 1889, the Ao tribe was formally annexed to British territory, all the villages officially visited, houses counted and revenue collected.

From 1876 we had lived in this land of hostilities without the protection of a Christian government. True, there was comparative safety when in 1885 this greater power declared there should be no more war; yet until this final act of incorporation into the Indian empire there was great unrest and distraction. Now, the earnest prayers of years were answered, and these mountain paths, so long tracked by cruelty and blood, were open for the coming of the messengers of the Prince of Peace.

XXII

THE NAGA HILL SUSPENSION BRIDGE

BETWEEN Molung and Amguri there were two rivers, and no bridges or boats at our command. The first, the Taero, was usually fordable, although ofttimes under the greatest difficulties; while to cross the broader Jhanzi our carriers were dependent upon a chance dugout (a small boat hewn out of a solid log), or a tea-garden elephant, and we were often cut off from our mail and needed supplies for a fortnight, a month, or even longer.

After long experiencing these difficulties, the country now having become more settled, Mr. Clark conceived the idea of spanning the Jhanzi, above its confluence with the Taero, by a wire suspension bridge. Representative men of Molung being consulted and the project explained so far as possible, they were more than delighted, and very readily and gladly pledged the labor of the village for the construction of the bridge. The cold season came, the wire arrived at Amguri from Calcutta, a point on the river was chosen, and the working force of the village turned out full of enthusiasm for the new enterprise.

A part of the laborers were detained to prepare the camp, while others were despatched to bring up the

128

NAGA HILL SUSPENSION BRIDGE

material. When they saw those coils and coils of
"only wire," they were discouraged, disheartened,
and disgusted. "How can the Sahib make a bridge
of only wire? Impossible, impossible!" they exclaimed over and over again. However, they backed
their loads, and with much grumbling and grunting
and tugging reached the camp, and casting down the
wire at Mr. Clark's feet declared this to be the end.
Dejection spread rapidly, and the whole camp sat for
a full half-day or longer murmuring and complaining.
When a Naga is depressed, disheartened, or in doubt,
it is almost impossible to move him. However, by
exercising some sternness and more moral suasion, the
men were brought to their feet. The stream was
spanned with a bridge of rafts to connect the two
shores, and the first suspension wire made fast to the
base of large trees on opposite banks.

The necessary number of wires having been strung,
and the tension carefully adjusted, next came the apparently perilous work of flooring this high structure.
Side wires were placed for guards, and to prevent the
bridge from swaying, stay wires, extending from it on
either side, were fastened high up in trees far away.
The entire party then mounted the bridge, and its
strength being clearly demonstrated to the satisfaction
of all, the forest rang with shouts of victory.

The bridge is two hundred feet span and forty feet
or more above high-water mark. It was never intended for animals, yet the Nagas do in emergency

drive over it their cows in taking them up from the plain. By occasionally renewing the bamboo floor, the bridge built in 1888 promises to last yet for many years.

Only a short distance below the bridge is a good ford in the dry season, and there soon followed a fine bridle path all the way from Molung to Amguri. A liberal grant from the English government gave us this path, as also the cost of the material for the bridge. The appreciation by the more remote villagers of this new and easier route added greatly to our opportunities of reaching the people.

Our English neighbors in the tea-gardens, interested and curious regarding this suspension bridge, invited us to join them there for a picnic. It was amusing to witness their undisguised wonder at the engineering skill of " only a missionary."

XXIII

REENFORCEMENTS

THE oft-repeated request for help in establishing a much-needed higher grade of school for training teachers and evangelists was answered in the coming of Rev. and Mrs. S. A. Perrine in 1892. We met on the Brahmaputra River en route to our Assam conference at Tura, in the Garo Hills. At this time I was taking what was generally conceded my final leave of Assam, but there lingered the deep conviction that this was not to be, and thus it proved when, with recuperated health and a joyous heart, I again joined my husband and the workers in the Naga Hills.

Mrs. Perrine writes as follows of her early attempt in starting a young people's society:

" The young people have taken hold splendidly, and we are greatly pleased that they are willing to lead and take part in the way suggested. Kilep, a son of one of the chief men of the village, led the first time under the new order. He was fearful that he would not speak ' proper words,' but finally consented to try. He was dressed in a comparatively clean blanket, and with tufts of new, clean, white cotton ornaments in his ears. It required much persuasion to induce him to stand up by the desk in front and face the people, but he finally did it, and with my help gave out the hymns and read the Scripture, made a very good talk and called upon several to lead in prayer.

"The next Sunday Bennie led the meeting. An American boy could not have done better. I sat near-by to help, but he conducted the services quite independently of me. In the 'conquest meeting' three stood up and told us about mission work in Sibsagor. Their willingness to do this was very encouraging. Afterwards six young people led in prayer, and the interest is very hopeful."

Mr. Perrine says: "A Naga prayer meeting *is* a prayer meeting. The Nagas come to pray, and they do what they come for. There are no long, killing pauses. All kneel during prayer, and at the conclusion join in the hearty 'amen.' I have been mightily impressed with the Naga amen.

"In our school the Bible is the text-book, with such other books as directly bear on the Bible. Our purpose is to so help any one of any tribe that, on going from this school to his own or another people, he can tell the 'old, old story.'"

In the school at Molung—and this has since been continued in the training school at Impur—it was decided to use the English language in connection with the vernaculars. As there were no books in the Naga Hills, save as the missionaries made them, it seemed desirable that the pupils be also educated in a tongue in which there were already text-books, and also that they have access to the entire Bible before it would be possible to translate it into the different tongues of the hills.

At the close of 1893 the mission force for the hill work was further augmented by the arrival of Rev. F. P. Haggard and family. There was not much spare room on the crest of Molung Hill for additional bungalows. Hence the school was moved into the chapel, and with some few additions and partitions easily accomplished by the Nagas with bamboos and mats, the schoolhouse was converted into a comfortable temporary dwelling for Mr. and Mrs. Haggard and their two children. In fact, all the houses of the missionaries were of temporary character, as previous to annexation to British territory no builders from Assam would come to us. The Nagas, with the help of the missionaries, were the architects.

For the benefit of those who think that missionaries live too luxuriously, we copy from Mr. Haggard's letters on his entrance upon the Ao Naga work. His letters also show how necessary all-around missionaries are for frontier fields.

" Possibly you would like to know why I have been so busy of late. We have been transforming an old schoolhouse into a dwelling, and since it was necessary to finish it before the rainy season began, we had to hurry. We are now fully installed, and I am writing upon my desk that I made from a box in which some of our goods came from America. Our kitchen table, washstand, bureau, cupboards, etc., have the same origin. You see, we do not care to put on any style here, but we are glad to be able to live happily and cosily and contentedly amid our surroundings, so different and with resources so much less than we had in America. Our house has three rooms and a storeroom, is built of rough-hewn posts, roof covered with grass, the side walls with two thicknesses of bamboo mats, the inner one finer and lighter than the outer. They are both woven by the Nagas, and afford only a partial protection from the cold."

Alluding to the millions stretching far back to Burma, Mr. Haggard further writes: "The thought of these vast hordes both inspires and discourages me. These people, when converted, have the same experience that we have at home. They sing 'Happy day that fixed my choice,' translated into their own tongue, and in prayer they come very near to the throne of grace. The trouble is, we missionaries are so few. We must be our own carpenters and builders, keep a large garden, have the care of goats and cows and ponies, mend our own shoes, saddles, and tinware; in short, because of our distance from civilization, must become 'jack of all trades.' The most earnest study of missions on your part will still fail to give you an adequate conception of the situation. It cannot be described by word or pen. One must see for himself, and then, like the Queen of Sheba, he will involuntarily exclaim, 'The half was not told me.'

MOKOKCHUNG POST-OFFICE

"While all seemed so strange at first, it is all so natural now that we feel perfectly at home. These people seem like our own brethren; we cannot repudiate their kinship. We must love them and give to them the bread of life. I never realized this so fully before. To the natural man these people would be revolting, but in Christ all is changed."

Since Molung was nearly at one extremity of the Ao tribe, we early began looking around toward the planting of a more central station. Such a site had already been chosen, subject to the approval of those who might join us. It was located between and near two large villages. In the tours of Mr. Clark and the native evangelists the gospel had been preached about there, but as yet these people would have none of it. Now, with this strong reenforcement of the mission, there came also redoubled energy and courage. New lines of work were inaugurated. Our long-projected plan was considered and its early execution entered upon with the hope of eventually reaching other tribes. From the beginning it was never contemplated stopping alone with these tribes bordering on the frontier; but on and on, conquering and to conquer, beyond and still beyond, until these mountains should be spanned and the kingdom of our Lord extended from the Brahmaputra to the Irawady, and from the Irawady to the Yangtse.

The proposed new site was visited and approved by the three missionaries, and steps were taken for the purchase of a considerable tract of land, sufficient for necessary bungalows, outhouses, and the no very distant Naga Hill Educational Institute, with dormitories. Some of the especially conservative old warriors were not in favor of having this new religion brought so near; others said, " It is taking too much land "; to others the price was a great temptation, and after annoying delays, with much parleying, the needful land was secured, about eighty acres, for eighty-two dollars.

Mr. Haggard says: " What a time we did have settling with them! All villages are little democracies, so the business must be done through a council, which we found very tedious, for they must talk, talk, talk. We consider the site an ideal one, being central to the tribe, near the great government bridle path, and only a few miles from government headquarters for the Ao tribe. We shall also be between two villages with an aggregate population of five thousand, and not far from others. It is a beautiful site, on the crest of the mountain."

Temporary, rude bamboo houses were put up, and occupied by the Perrines and Haggards in the autumn of 1894. Of the removal and settling in these temporary homes, Mr. Perrine writes: " The new station is from thirty to thirty-five miles south of Molung, but as far in time and hardships as from Chicago to San Francisco. If you don't know how much ' stuff ' you have, move to the Naga Hills, and you will find out. It is a big job to load up hundreds of coolies, a bigger one to

Mission Bungalow at Impur

get them started off, and a still larger work to pay them off and get rid of them. Oh, the wrangling and parleying! A Naga will sit and argue and parley as long as one will listen and answer him. Life in the jungles of this frontier is a Swiss Family Robinson sort of life with variations. Mrs. Haggard asked, 'Where in all the world are there people who do so many kinds of work as we?' while Mrs. Clark often remarks, 'It is a chore to live in the Naga Hills.' There is plenty of rough work, and plenty of play for one's wits in order to adapt means to an end, and use a wild and crude people.

" Napalese sawyers were gotten here to saw the lumber for the bungalows. Nagas had no such instruments, neither did they know how to use them, but as many as two hundred in one day brought lumber on their backs from the forest, from two to four miles distant. Chinese carpenters, under the direction of Mr. Dring, of the Garo mission, built the bungalows, and we all worked as general helpers at all trades. The missionaries agreed that a native or a semi-native house for a missionary does not pay; it costs more in the end in time and means than a permanent house, and is in no way satisfactory. Let no one get the impression that all of our surroundings are ideally perfect—that we have no trials, no strain on our patience, and what is more, nothing to test our faith and Christian character."

XXIV

WHITE RIBBONERS

MR. CLARK and I tarried at Molung upwards of a year after the Perrines and Haggards removed to Impur, and our remaining at this, our old, first home among these people, was amply rewarded.

I quote from a letter written at this period: " A religious and social reform has been quietly going on at Molung, beginning with a young man, who, strengthened by the Holy Spirit and helped by Assamese teacher Zilli, laid hold of one of his companions, and by persistent, prayerful effort brought him to Christ. Here were now two promising young men, the pick of the village, educated in the school, one, the son of our most influential village official, and the hearts of both filled with the love of Jesus, and set for the defense of his kingdom and social purity. Every form of demon worship, open or suspected, was attacked—Sunday-breaking, rice-beer drinking, licentiousness, and all social vices. One after another of the young people were pressed into the ranks, and the White Ribbon Society, without the name, or buttonholes in which to wear the badge, grew in numbers and influence and power. Instead of congregating promiscuously at different houses to sleep at night, singing objectionable songs,

138

telling doubtful stories, and engaging in lewd conversation, these young reformers separated themselves and built a dormitory for their own accommodation, in which purity and holiness should reign. Here at morning and evening time the voice of prayer and songs of praise are heard. A note received from one of my schoolboys, proud of his English, tells me of his interest in the Christian Endeavor meeting, and that he and one of his schoolmates 'will ask last Sunday before the church to baptize.'

"As the harvest time approached, with the accustomed reaping in 'bees,' with more or less drinking and feasting, we were solicitous for these young Christians. But prayers prevailed, and through these days of trial they came forth unscathed. When called to work where the rice-beer was served, these withdrew from the crowd and ate their midday meal by themselves; and when they called the neighbors to harvest their crops no beer was served. If a pig were to furnish the meal where these 'white ribboners' worked, they insisted upon its being killed in the village, lest, if slain on the field, suspicious persons might construe it as secretly appeasing a cultivation deity, and they would have none of this. On returning one morning from our woman's early prayer meeting—and where are trysts with Christ more precious?—I met old Mopoimba scolding and storming through the village, saying he had never seen things on this wise before. He couldn't get any one to carry his live pig to the harvest field; it must be killed first; even his own boys (two were among the reformers) would not serve him.

"Prayer meetings have been called for the sick, and there has been no small stir among the diviners and soothsayers, who are fast losing their gains. Our chapel has been filled, all the religious services well sustained; there have been adult prayer meetings, young people's prayer meetings, children's prayer meetings, and street preaching. The older Christians have been in sympathy with the movement, renewing their covenant vows, and during the cold season sixty new converts have been baptized. The examinations are thorough, and the knowledge evinced of the fundamental principles of Christianity is unusually satisfactory. Total abstinence from all intoxicants is required. One of our young reformers has his house built and is all ready to receive his intended bride, but he will not marry her until she promises—and practises too—to give up rice-beer drinking.

"Our last harvest home festival showed the largest amount of rice ever brought in on such an occasion. It was sold for fourteen rupees, almost five dollars. As we congratulated the people on being able to contribute so much more now than in the old war days, one replied, 'Why, yes, in the old war days, before we knew the only true God and our new-found King Jesus, and kept his Sabbath, we scarcely saw a pice. With so many heavy war indemnities, guards to be maintained about the village and on the cultivation, and costly

ON A PREACHING TOUR

sacrifices for the old demon worship, we were half starved.'

" Our people tell us that many times they had only one good meal a day, which they took in the morning, cheating their stomachs at night, as they said, ' when sleep would cause us to forget our hunger.' "

XXV

FIRST RALLY OF CHRISTIAN CLANS

THE first rally of the churches was held at Molung in 1897. Mr. and Mrs. Haggard having entered upon the work in the Lhota tribe, a long way removed, were unable to be present. The first to arrive after a three days' march were Mr. and Mrs. Perrine, with baby Linden, four months old, in a basket on a Naga's back; and their preachers, helpers, and load-carriers; then came representatives from other churches, until every available shelter on our compound was brought into requisition, but the hospitality of the village was sufficient for the accommodation of all.

The first day of the Association was ushered in with a severe March storm. During the previous night the winds howled and roared, while the old mat bungalow trembled and shook until we arose from our beds to be prepared for whatsoever might happen. The morning dawn found the occupants of the bungalow all right, but the house was in terrible disorder. The roof on one side was lifted, and the litter from old mats and bamboos and decaying thatch was everywhere; yet this seemed a small matter, when it was discovered that an opening had been made in our fowl-house and the "association fatted calf," chickens, and ducks had been

142

feasted on by tiger-cats, leaving but two out of twenty-eight. In a place where there are no markets this was decidedly disappointing. But the end was not yet; less than twenty-four hours passed when ten cows and calves from our herd were found scattered in the jungle, victims of tigers. One cow, giving less than one quart of milk a day, was alone spared us wherewith to entertain our guests.

Still further trials awaited us. There came messengers from our government demanding promptly the services of our people, and we greatly feared the breaking up of our long-anticipated associational meetings. The missionaries finally decided to take the responsibility of detaining our men for a few days; a note to this effect was speedily despatched to the English officer and the request was cheerfully granted. This matter settled, the first evening of the meeting was devoted to conference and prayer.

The following morning the first subject on the programme was prayer. Other topics were evangelization, the Holy Spirit, Christian benevolence, shall the Nagas bury their dead? should all Christians learn to read? by what changes in food, houses, sanitation, and clothing shall Christians better their mode of living?

We were very pleasantly surprised by the spirit, animation, earnestness, and even ability with which these questions were handled, especially by some just out of the darkness of heathenism. The last subject may differ somewhat from those considered in like home gatherings; some costume, a little more cloth, was recommended.

The matter of disposing of the dead was well discussed and burial approved, rather than enclosing the body in a miniature leaf-house placed on an elevated platform. Only four days later there came a practical test of this decision in the death of little Pee-tor (Peter), the name chosen from the Scriptures for the firstborn of our young Naga pastor, Kilep. The Christians gathered at the house for prayer; a small box was provided, the little form placed therein, religious services held at the chapel, when followed the first burial of the dead in all these mountain villages.

It was decided to hold these associational meetings annually, and the Yazang church extended a very cordial invitation for the next year. Immediately following these meetings, a teachers' and preachers' institute was conducted by Mr. Perrine with much profit. The first Sabbath after these meetings two persons from another village were baptized. A good religious interest continued and upward of twenty new names were enrolled on our church book.

XXVI

MOLUNG TO IMPUR

OUR Assamese helper, Zilli, had been ordained and placed over the church at Molung; a Naga young man was chosen and supported by the church as his assistant in pastoral and school work. The Christian element of the village now seemed fully competent to care for the spiritual and temporal interests here, and it was thought best that the missionary force should all be gathered at Impur, leaving this little Christian colony to walk alone.

With full hearts we took leave of our old, first home among this people, where we had spent so many happy and anxious days. The final Sabbath was a blessed day. Meetings for the examination of candidates for baptism were held on Friday and Saturday evenings, and on Sunday morning twenty-seven arose from the baptismal waters to newness of life. How could we but thank God that he had permitted us to come hither? At this time my journal reads:

" To tear ourselves away from these, our very own in the Lord, is indeed heart-breaking, and we believe too that the people are sincere in their expressions of grief. The chapel on this last Sabbath was trimmed with foliage and flowers, and was filled with people

K   145 both morning and evening, while many were at the door unable to gain entrance. Special services were arranged by the Christians, in which many took part. The prayers were earnest and touching; we cried and the people cried, tears coursing down the hardened cheeks of old-time warriors unused to weep."

Everything possible was done to help us on our way. Men volunteered as load-carriers; village officials honored us by their presence for a considerable distance; women and children affectionately accompanied us to the next neighboring village; there were young men too, going along to the Impur Training School. With our loads, many and exceedingly diverse, and with flocks and herds, we reached Impur the third day, and were joyously welcomed and entertained by our missionary associates. We had left much; we had come to much.

Impur is an ideal, picturesque location, a little over four thousand feet altitude, with pretty rolling lands, and a little eminence for each of the three bungalows. From our crest we look on peaks and peaks beyond, six thousand, eight thousand, even ten thousand feet elevation, from which the waters course Burma-ward. The missionaries named the place Impur, meaning in Naga dialect chieftown, a center, from which even now the light of the Cross is shining afar.

Impur is one hundred miles from Kohima, the headquarters of British rule in the Naga hills, and about ten miles from Mokokchung, the subdivisional head-

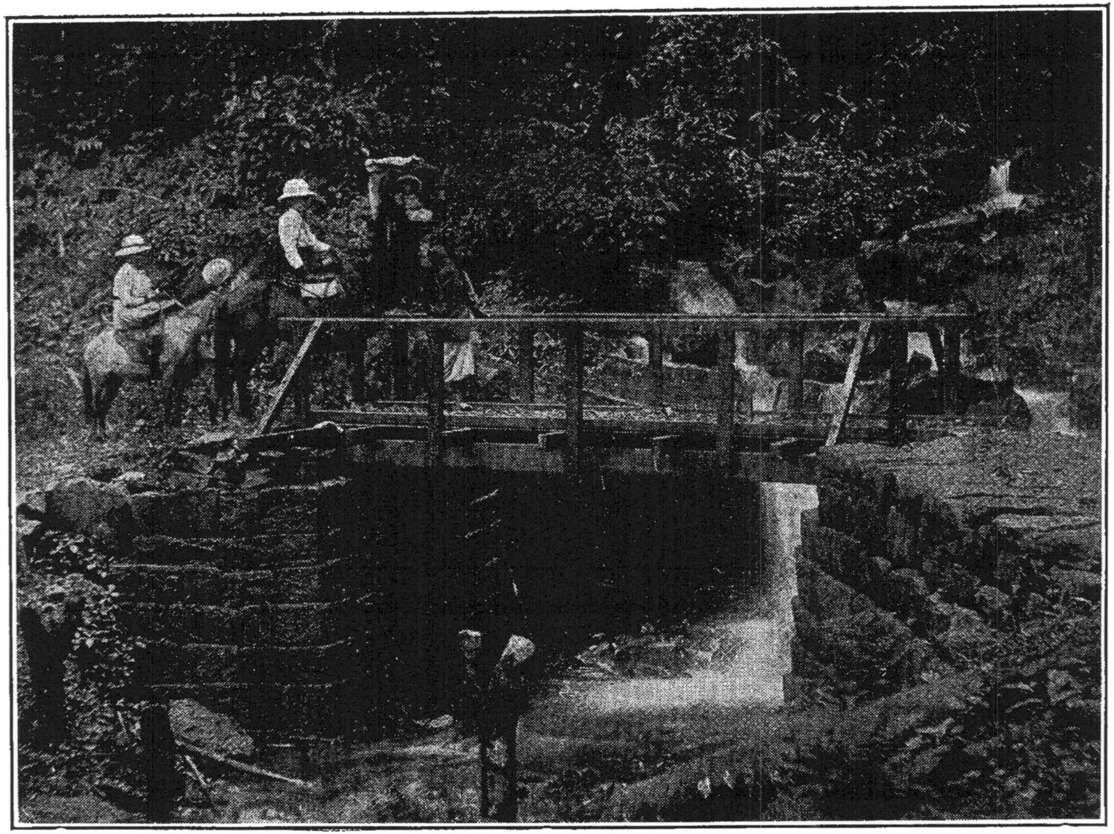

Page 147 A GOVERNMENT BRIDLE PATH

quarters, where one English officer with a native police force is located. Our little mission oasis hears from
the outer world by government mail every two days (at
present writing a daily mail). Following the main
mountain ridges, a fine bridle path with a grade of " one
in ten " has been constructed from Kohima via Wokha
and Mokokchung to a military post in the plain, about
one hundred and sixty miles. Impur is only two miles
from this grand trunk line. From Impur to Moriani,
our nearest station in the plain, is about fifty miles.

Along these routes are very comfortable rest-houses,
separated by easy day's marches. These houses are
furnished with tables, chairs, and bedsteads, where the
traveler may find lodging, bringing with him his own
bedding, food, crockery, and cooking utensils. Government and the mission jointly have also improved old
paths along other lines and made them possible for
ponies, thus enabling the missionary now to ride
through a considerable portion of his parish.

There was soon gathered at Impur quite a little
community of Christian workers. A little church was
organized, and the place became a real beehive of earnest, consecrated work. Mr. Haggard taught the
preachers how to preach and visited among the villages, looking after the churches and giving the gospel
to the heathen. Mrs. Haggard, in addition to assisting
her husband and caring for her own Roy, Hattie, and
Harold, had an important part in this school work. The
click, click of her sewing-machine, run by an Assamese

under her superintendence, sounded very civilized and businesslike on these far-away mountaintops, promising much as an elevating influence in clothing those who were gradually coming to realize their present insufficiency.

Mr. Clark devoted himself more especially to his Naga-English dictionary and translation work. Mr. and Mrs. Perrine were over the Training School, preparing young men for pastors, evangelists, and day-school teachers, and young women to be suitable wives for such men. The school opened with nine pupils; it soon numbered sixty; upwards of ninety were last reported.

Our school and chapel building was a rude structure and the seats ruder still, but through the kindness of a special gift, added to contributions by the missionaries, we soon had a fine, modern-seated house. There are dormitories for the boys, and the widow of our lamented Zilli is matron for the girls. Boys and girls whose parents do not support them work a part of each day to pay for their rice and schooling. The pupils studying in this Training School are, many of them, sons and daughters of old-time head-cutters, who still carry their decorated spears and battle-axes and wear insignia emblematical of bloody deeds.

While each missionary had his own department, there were frequent conferences, to which each one brought his encouragements and perplexities. We laughed and were glad as in one of these gatherings the

IMPUR TRAINING-SCHOOL PUPILS

Page 149

head of the Training School, in referring to the merits of his different pupils, declared that "the young man from Waramong is a 'clipper from away back.'"

Imonungshi, a most unpromising fellow, given to drink and with an expressionless face, was asked by Mrs. Perrine if he would paint the house. He began, but soon it seemed as if he had mistaken his orders. Such a sight! Hair, arms, and legs alike were covered with a good share of the contents of the paint pail. He had been repeatedly labored with for his drunken sprees, but insisted that the habit was uncontrollable. However, as Mr. Perrine entered the schoolroom one morning, behold Imo was there at his a, b, c's. Mr. Perrine tried to dissuade him from this seemingly useless attempt, as he had, up to this time, appeared unusually dull. But a new light was now in his eyes, a fixed and holy purpose in his savage heart, and he said: "Teacher, I'll come to school forty years if necessary to learn to read." Together they knelt in prayer, and since, with Christ as his Master, Imo has gone on from strength to strength. He attended school regularly, and in due time was chosen pastor of the Impur church. His first sermon was five minutes long, and he had to be prompted in his Scripture reading. Behold what hath God wrought!

AMONG THE LHOTAS

R EV. W. E. WITTER and wife arriving in Assam in 1884, full of American rush and speed, were soon prostrated from overwork at Sibsagor.

> It is not well for the Christian white
> To hustle the Aryan brown,
> For the Christian writhes and the Aryan smiles
> And weareth the Christian down.

The more invigorating climate of the Naga Hills was suggested, and Wokha village, in the Lhota tribe, a commanding situation forty-four hundred feet above sea-level was selected. English political control had just been extended over this tribe, and a subdivisional officer with a native military force was in command, making this a comparatively safe place for mission work. A bridle path to the plains made Wokha accessible, rendering still more desirable this connecting link between the Angamis and Aos. With Kohima, sixty miles southwest, already occupied, also Molung, ninety miles northeast, a grand trunk line of missions to the Nagas would thus be opened. The importance of an early occupation of this field had already been pressed upon the Missionary Union.

Rev. P. H. Moore, of Nowgong, and Mr. Witter,

therefore, visited Molung to consult about this matter. Mr. Witter thus relates the outcome of that conference: " The year 1885 found the Lhotas still unprovided for. Brother Clark, however, believing that God was unmistakably calling upon us to enter this field without delay, after taking a few rapid, nervous paces across the trembling bamboo floor of his rude house at Molung, exclaimed: 'If the Witters will occupy Wokha at once the expense of their transfer shall be met.' Accordingly a telegram was sent to the Deputy Commissioner of the Naga Hills asking permission to open a mission station among the Lhotas. The reply was favorable, an old, abandoned rest-house was placed at our disposal, and March 31, 1885, our first dear home with its blessed memories of work among the Assamese and Kohls was left, and a tea estate near the foot of the hills was reached April 7th. Here we were met by Rev. C. D. King, of Kohima, who had traveled one hundred and twenty miles on foot to help us on our new and untried way. Mr. King was accompanied by several native police and a hundred Naga coolies."

Mrs. Witter writes: " The first part of our march was in the plains through dense jungle. Mr. King and Mr. Witter took turns riding our pony and tramping. I was mounted on an old gray pony. We found the frail bamboo bridges very treacherous, and suddenly I felt my pony sinking beneath me. Mr. King snatched me from the saddle, only to lose me in water almost beyond my depth. But I soon touched bottom, and almost as quickly was dragged to the shore, thoroughly drenched. The pony escaped with only a sprain.

" The next day's march was up and down hills along a narrow path, one side of which was flanked by a perpendicular wall of rock, and on the other side one could look down, down, hundreds of feet. We had beautiful bits of scenery, and the ever-shifting lights and shadows on the hillsides. The last day's journey convinced me that, until then, I knew nothing of Naga hill roads. We had come to one of the short cuts, a genuine Naga path, over which these men delight in clambering, requiring hands as well as feet.

" After many varied and exciting experiences Wokha station was reached. Our only white neighbor is the subdivisional officer, who occupies another rude rest-house. We have only two rooms, mud walls, earth floor, so dirty the mud falls off, the dirt sifts through the walls, and there is no ceiling, only the grass roof over our heads. The bamboos are so full of boring insects that a white powder is constantly falling, and the large colony of rats is as much at home as are we. For our pantry we have a couple of boxes, with shelves, curtained. Our wardrobe is but a rope, over which we hang our clothes. It is a puzzling question where to store all of our things. This miserable little hut is too insecure to withstand the fierce winds and fearful rains, and we are seriously considering an outlay of from twenty to thirty dollars for a new house, as a necessity for health and comfort through the long rainy season

GOVERNMENT REST-HOUSE

Page 153

just at hand. A new language is to be acquired, and there is not a letter, not one Christian person, not one who has ever heard the name of Jesus. The many sepoys and sepoys' children here understand Assamese, and we are finding that our stay in Sibsagor was greatly to our advantage. Our use of the Assamese tongue enables us to begin work at once, and we have a little school in Assamese and religious services every Sabbath. But our hearts are not at rest. The Nagas swarm about us on every hand, and we are making pundits of our servants. We do love these wild people. Our Naga boys are interesting us more and more; they creep right into our hearts. Every day we are so glad we are here. It will be a pleasure to work among these people if we are permitted to remain."

Mr. Witter's health improved much by the bracing mountain air, and there was joy and gladness and hope in this happy little mountain eyrie, " busy, busy all the time." In less than a year it became necessary to make the long, hard journey of sixty miles to Kohima for medical attendance. As soon as it was deemed prudent they set out again for Wokha, with tiny, seven-weeks-old Volney in a snug little canopied box on a Naga's back, returning, as Mrs. Witter said, " with a little hindering helper."

By some change in the English officials a large government rest-house was offered them free of rent, which, with the doors and windows Mr. Witter had already provided for a new house, made them very comfortable without the expense in money and time of building. Their organ and stove had been gotten up from Sibsagor, adding much to their pleasure and comfort. The organ proved very useful in the work and amused the Nagas greatly.

But a dark cloud was fast forming over this happy, hopeful horizon. There was no uncertain warning in the failing health of both Mr. and Mrs. Witter, and the latter was taken to the hospitable mission bungalow at Nowgong, Assam, where she might receive proper medical aid and nursing. Mr. Witter, in response to recent inquiries, says: " We left Assam in the spring of 1888. Mrs. Witter never returned to the mountains after the birth of Marjorie, and Marjorie was six months old when I first saw her. I remained on at Wokha alone until I was so reduced in health as to be unable to pack up and go to Kohima, so Brother Rivenburg came over and packed my things for me and took me to his home, where I remained several months and completed the outline grammar of the Lhota Naga language, with a vocabulary which was published by the government of India, appearing in print just two days before we left for America. Aside from the grammar we made typewritten primers, from which our Lhota boys learned to read, and Mrs. Witter translated the Assamese catechism into Lhota, and it was she who began the first formal teaching of divine truth to this people. She also translated the first hymn, ' There is a Happy Land.' Afterward I translated several hymns, the hymns, were sent to Mr. Haggard when he began his work among the Lhotas. Mrs. Witter has always thought that one or two of the boys whom she taught to sing, and to whom she so repeatedly told the story of the Saviour, did really pass out of death into life, but they were young and under the control of pagan parents."

For several years circumstances prevented further mission work among the Lhotas. Rev. F. P. Haggard, while among the Aos at Impur, visited much among the Lhota villages, and with his family lived at Wokha portions of the years 1896-1897, and was greatly encouraged in the prosecution of the work. While there he wrote: "Two Lhota pundits have been secured and much time will be spent in the study of the language. It is nearly ten years since the Witters closed their short but eventful and profitable labors at Wokha. They are well remembered by the people. The seed sowed will yet bring forth fruit. I am now able to join with my boys in a couple of hymns that I have made. We can also repeat a version of the Lord's Prayer in Lhota. A daily service is inspiring to us all. The people seem thoroughly interested, and I have reason to believe that some, at least, of this interest is not wholly ephemeral. I am especially pleased with the persistent desire of so many to learn."

The Missionary Union, however, being straitened financially, asked the Haggards to return to the work at Impur, and thus the Lhotas were a second time left without gospel heralds.

In December, 1896, Zilli, our Assamese preacher and teacher among the Aos, was appointed to this work. He visited the field and made all arrangements for the removal of his family to Wokha, when he was suddenly taken ill, and on Christmas Day with aching, disappointed hearts we followed his body to the open grave in our little cemetery at Impur.

Later Robi, an Assamese worker at Impur, was sent to Wokha and was received by the people with many expressions of favor. A very hopeful feature of our work among the Lhotas is that for the past few years there have been Lhota boys, and more recently several Lhota girls, in the Impur Training School, a number of whom have been baptized. One of these boys has already been preaching among his people. Boys from the Sema tribe, which borders on the Lhota, have also attended the school at Impur, whence go evangelists, pastors, and school-teachers to herald the gospel message in many villages of these savage tribes. A fairly strong church has been established among the Lhotas at Okotsa.

XXVIII

"THE Arthington Aborigines Mission" was an organization sustained largely by Mr. Arthington, an English gentleman of the Society of Friends. He was a large giver to missions, his contribution being always for pioneer work, with instructions that only two workers go to a place, learn the language, give the gospel to the people, then move on to other fields, not tarrying to perpetuate their work.

In 1895 Rev. William Pettigrew, of this mission, having applied for admittance to the Missionary Union, opened a station in 1896 at Ukhrul, among the Tangkhul Nagas, in Manipur. This is nominally an independent State, but until the ascension to the throne of its now minor raja (king) is subject to the government of Assam. The population of this State approaches three hundred thousand, and Mr. Pettigrew, while not permitted to give religious instruction to the Manipuris proper, has done good service along educational lines, serving as government inspector of schools.

The labors of this lone worker and his wife have been greatly blessed among the Tangkhuls. Already a goodly number of young men of this savage tribe have openly confessed Christ and are exercising a

strong influence in favor of the missionary and his message. Schools have been established and churches
organized. Mr. Pettigrew has put several school text-
books through the press, a hymn-book, and translations
of Luke, John, and the Acts of the Apostles.

A Garo Christian baptized by Dr. Bronson, formerly
of the Assam mission, is medical compounder at the
capital, Manipur, and renders some assistance to the
missionary. Thus the fruits of the faithful labors of
our crowned ones are being gathered.

Mr. Pettigrew writes: " There is no record of the
gospel being introduced or any missionary entering
this interesting and beautiful country up to the end of
1893. William Carey and his associates at Serampore
(India) evidently came in touch with some Manipuris, for we have the whole New Testament translated
into their language and printed by the press at Serampore in 1824. There is only one known copy of this
work, and that is in the library of the British and
Foreign Bible Society, London."

The opening of this mission is a long link in the
chain extending across these hills from Assam, via
Kohima and Manipur, to Burma.

After a much-needed furlough in England the Petti-
grews have now returned to Manipur, Mr. Pettigrew
further equipped for effective mission work by the
study of medicine.

XXIX

HOMEWARD BOUND

THE happy circle at Impur, full of work and glad anticipations, was broken in February, 1899, by the return to America of Mr. and Mrs. Haggard and their three children. Their furlough over, while en-route to Assam they were recalled from London by the Missionary Union to meet an emergency in the home service in which they have since been engaged. This was a great disappointment to them personally and a severe blow to the Naga Hill Mission. Mr. Haggard, first an assistant secretary, then editorial, is now one of the Corresponding Secretaries of the Missionary Union.

Soon Mr. and Mrs. Perrine sailed for the homeland and Mr. Clark and I were again left alone so far as missionary associates were concerned. We toured among the villages, visiting churches and schools, and carried the gospel to hundreds of pagan warriors, my bearer now a pony instead of relays of strong Nagas.

Soon after the arrival of Rev. and Mrs. Dowd, in 1901, the word rapidly spread to distant villages that Mr. Clark and I were about to leave the hills, perhaps finally. The people came in swarms to see us, and old-time warriors pleaded, " Father, why will you go? Is there not some place in this country where the Mem Sahib can get well?" "But we have told you again and again of the one Supreme Rajah and you have not heeded. Why should we stay longer?" Then came the piteous answer, "Yes, we have grown old in the bad way, but we want our children to be better. We are all so much happier and more prosperous under this reign of peace. Oh, do not leave us!" February 28, 1901, will we ever—can we ever—forget it?

We were five days on ponies in reaching the plain, nearing which a chorus of many voices singing in Assamese greeted our ears, and soon in the little rest-house at the foot of the hills we were taking tea with these welcoming Christians from the tea-gardens. An English planter and his wife drove up; others from near-by gardens called, while quartered in the one other room of the little rest-house was our own missionary, Rev. O. L. Swanson, from Golaghat.

The next morning, six miles by dog-cart brought us to Moriani, then twenty-five miles "narrow gage" to the Brahmaputra, and five days later we reached the city of palaces, Calcutta. En route down the Brahmaputra we were met by Doctor and Mrs. Rivenburg and their one "flower," Narola, twelve years of age, whom they committed to our charge—a sacred trust—while they turned back to their lonely home in the far-away mountains. Is this the romance of missions? Let those who think so try it.

Less than a half-day's journey from Calcutta, in the

MAIL STEAMER ON BRAHMAPUTRA RIVE

treacherous Hoogly, our steamer suddenly lurched, and from our submerged cabin it was with great difficulty that I was rescued. Great excitement prevailed lest the grounded vessel sink and all be lost. In due time, however, all the passengers were conveyed to a steam launch, some drenched and all baggageless, and returned to Calcutta.

Our second embarkation was on the old-established steamship line, the " P. and O.," from which we landed safely in old England. Then just a little " run across," and home, home, home! If you want to know the meaning of that dear word be a missionary.

XXX

WHEN we entered " A Corner of India " the darkness seemed impenetrable. Lo, the morning breaketh! Then " Stay out " was the rallying cry of savage warriors. Now " Come and welcome " is the ringing call to the young men and women of America who are saying, " Here am I, send me." Glorious harvests await the reapers. Eleven little churches, approaching eight hundred members, and our splendid training school proclaim the hastening day. The work fascinates one. " The doctor's orders have broken my heart," wrote Mrs. Perrine just previous to leaving with her husband for America, 1905. " Do you know the Naga Hills and the people were never so attractive to me? It seems as if I could not leave them. There is just one place for me, and that is right here among the Nagas. There is so much to do; we are all so busy. Mr. Perrine's office is a perfect beehive from 7.30 A. M. to 4 P. M. We are making books in the Sema and Lhota languages."

" After many years of siege and storming," writes Mrs. Dowd, " the chief fort has been taken, Lungkum, the largest village in the Ao tribe, and one which has longest withstood our battering rams. The smaller

162

villages have been saying, 'When Lungkum becomes Christian, then we will.' A boy from our training school became a Christian, married a Christian girl, and returned to this village to teach and to preach. Now the head man professes to have accepted the new religion and has come to ask that baptism be administered to him in his own village as a witness to neighbors and friends of his allegiance to 'King Jesus.' He came for this interview dressed in all his old war finery, covered with symbols of heads of enemies he had brought to his village."

The reception of my husband by this village on his return to the Naga Hills in 1904 was truly royal and in striking contrast with his first visit, nineteen years previous, when accompanying an English military expedition necessitated by these warlike people. Doctor Clark is now devoting himself principally to literary work, always in such demand when savage hearts are tamed and eager for the knowledge that makes for righteousness. Now, with the gospel well entrenched among the Aos, with several Christian communities among the Lhotas, the promise of an early break among the powerful and numerous Semas, and farther on the work already going forward among the Angamis and Tangkhuls, the eye of faith can easily foresee the joyful greetings of the frontier heralds of the cross in Assam as they clasp hands with those from Burma on some one of those mountain crests and shout, " Oh, clap your hands, all ye people ; shout unto Jehovah with the voice of triumph, for the Lord most high is terrible; He is a great King over all the earth."

Yes, "On and still on" must be our watchword, for not only can we see this blessed meeting and hear this joyful cry from the borders of Assam and Burma, but even now the Missionary Union is re-establishing the work at Sadiya in the persons of Reverend and Mrs. Jackman, and thus on to Tibet must hasten the banner of glad tidings, until our missionaries from Assam, marching through western China, plant the cross among the Tibetans in realization of the visions of the sainted Judsons, Browns, Cutters, Kincaids, and many other inspired heralds of the kingdom.

"Watchman, what of the night? The morning cometh!"

———

To complete our story and bring it up to date we add the following few flashlights from several of these mountain heights:

IMPUR: Mr. Dowd sends the inspiring word that the number of baptisms on the Impur field has been three times that for the previous five years. In 1905 there were recorded one hundred and ninety-one baptisms, and in 1906 one hundred and thirty-eight. The churches have (in 1906) a membership of seven hundred and sixty, nearly half of whom have been gathered within the past two years. Although Mr. and Mrs. Perrine have had to

Page 164   YOUNG EVANGELIST AND HIS WIFE

retire permanently from the country on account of Mrs. Perrine's health, Doctor and Mrs. Loops and Mr. and Mrs. Longwell have gone out to strengthen the station.

In January, 1896, Doctor Clark reported the Gospels of Matthew and John as nearly ready for printing, while a year later Mr. Dowd completed a translation of Mark. New arrangements have been made by which the government Educational Department takes over the village schools, thus far without seriously affecting the faithfulness of the teachers as Christian leaders. Such government inspection unquestionably stimulates both teachers and pupils to greater thoroughness, while at the same time it places at the disposal of the mission the experience and advice of trained educational leaders and diminishes financial burdens by " grants-in-aid."

The little band of Christians at Lungkun has found a consecrated and influential helper in Toshikaba, one of the village chief men who was baptized last January. He is said to have killed ten men and brought home their heads to the village in his earlier days. At Jakpa, on the border, Yangchu, a chief man, was recently baptized, the first-fruits of the warlike Moyung tribe. He was present at the Association this year and made his offering to the foreign mission fund that had been the means of his conversion. . . . The opportunities in this field are great, and the people accessible. Hearts long resistant are being softened. Whole villages after years of hostility or indifference are giving attention to the preaching of the word.

KOHIMA: Doctor and Mrs. Rivenburg returned to America for their second furlough late in 1905, after a term of eleven years' continuous service, leaving the work to Mr. and Mrs. Dickson, who had been designated to Kohima. When Doctor Rivenburg left, there were eighty young people in the station school, five of them girls. A year later Mr. Dickson reported a further increase of boys. The membership of the little church has doubled in three years.

The evangelists report a greatly changed attitude of the Angamis toward the gospel. The people are listening and inquiring concerning Christianity as never before. A number of the older schoolboys have given up heathen worship. Three new schools have been opened, one of them in the largest Sema Naga village, which is on the Angami border. Recently a Christian Angami returned from the Burma side, where he had been trading, with a letter from Doctor East of Haka, impressing anew our nearness to other peoples; yet the hills intervening are swarming with savages waiting to hear the message of salvation.

UKHRUL: Among the twenty thousand Tangkhul Nagas, northeast of the capital of Manipur, Mr. Pettigrew is laying the foundations of a new order of things. He turned to them when forbidden by the Manipur government to work among Manipuris or to live in their capital city, and these savage head-hunters have received him cordially. He is probably the only white man who speaks their language, which he has reduced to writing. The Gospels of Luke and John, and the Acts have been translated.

The two schools have increased to eleven, with a little over three hundred pupils, only five of whom are girls. Seventy of the three hundred are in the station school in Ukhrul. The five native evangelists are making good use of their knowledge of medical and minor surgical treatment, and a hospital dispensary is now being erected at headquarters. There is only one church thus far, and that numbers but twenty-nine members, half of whom were baptized last year. The evangelists report (1906) some thirty more awaiting the ordinance. The members have built a meeting-house in the center of the village, where crowds gather Tuesday and Friday evenings, as well as on Sunday. There are nearly a hundred pupils in the station Sunday-school, besides Sunday-school classes in the station schools.

SADIYA: Here Rev. and Mrs. L. W. B. Jackman are giving their first attention to Abors and Miris, who are allied tribes. The Abors, who inhabit the mountains, are the most powerful tribe on this frontier, and are estimated at two hundred thousand. The Miris of the plains are somewhat Hinduized. No church has been formed yet, and the six baptized in 1906 were from other tribes, but it is hoped that a church organization will soon be perfected. The earnestness and Christian spirit manifested by the new Christians have been a great source of encouragement. Requests from the head men of several Abor villages for medical attendance will now be responded to by Doctor Kirby who, with his wife, has joined the mission force at Sadiya. The Miris are asking for schools, and teachers for this new opening must be trained. With building and other manifold labors Mr. Jackman has worked steadily upon the language of the Abor-Miri people, and has already several manuscripts ready for the press. " The loving Father has most wonderfully kept us. Dangers have come near, but the Master was nearer to ward them off and little harm has come to us."

My husband thus expresses the changes wrought in these mountain wilds:

" Thirty years ago I took up residence in these Naga hills in a village where some work had been done by a native evangelist. Save at this place, over all these ranges of hills hung the black pall of heathen, barbaric darkness. Now from some twenty of the fifty or more villages crowning the mountain crests floats the glorious banner of Christ, held by his Naga disciples. The softening twilight of Christianity is here. Soon the broad daylight with its transforming power will reveal a Christianized people."

Deacidified using the Bookkeeper process
Neutralizing agent Magnesium Oxide
Treatment Date Sept 2005

PreservationTechnologies
A WORLD LEADER IN PAPER PRESERVATION
111 Thomson Park Drive
Cranberry Township, PA 16066
(724) 779-2111